GRACE

SECOND EDITION

FOR THOSE WHO THINK THEY DON'T MEASURE UP

BOB LENZ

GRACE

Originally published by Destiny Image Publishers, Inc., 2008

2nd Edition published by Life Promotions, Inc.,
Appleton, Wisconsin, 2016

ISBN: 978-0-9856716-6-2 Paperback
ISBN: 978-0-9856716-7-9 e-book

Library of Congress Control Number: 2016938874

Printed in the United States of America

Life Promotions, Inc.

4 North Systems Drive, Suite C
Appleton, Wisconsin 54914
info@lifepromotions.com

DEDICATION

I dedicate this book to my mom and dad:

Jan (Verhagen) Lenz, 1936-1999. Loved well.

Dave Lenz, 1933-2000. No regrets.

Mom, thanks for believing in me when I felt like I didn't
measure up. I can still hear you cheering me on when I
want to quit.

Dad, thank you for your unconditional love.
You taught me what really matters in life.

I wish you two were still here, and not just because you'd buy
the first 1,000 copies of this book.

Love you always,
Bob

ACKNOWLEDGEMENTS

How do I begin to thank all the people who have had an impact in making this book a reality? Relationship is what matters. Because of that, many of you have had an impact on me. Thank you for being a part of my life. I'd like to highlight a few:

My wife and best friend, Carol. I still see Jesus in you. Thanks for listening to me, living with me, loving me, challenging me, gracing me, and enjoying me. I'm starting to believe it. My children, Amber, Danielle, David, Joyel, and Timothy. I love you. You bring life to my life.

Bill and James for being my brothers, friends, and co-laborers. I feel supported by your love. Tim and Lois for modeling perfect grace. The Mav family for showing me grace and community. Steve and Lynda for faithfully standing with me. Carla for learning to receive. AJ—here it is…finally. Thanks for your encouragement. Stan, you've made a difference.

My Life Promotions family, the staff, Board, supporters, volunteers, prayer partners, staff members who have moved on, and friends of youth. Thanks for the grace needed in teamwork. *"That they may know Him"* (see John 17:3).

Christ the Rock Community Church—a place to come home to, worship with, and be sent out of by grace. All the people I have had the privilege of teaming up with to share the good news of the Gospel. My circle of friends at Youth Encounter.

Friends at Compassion International. Let's keep loving Jesus by loving kids. Father Paul Feider who walked me through the dark side of grace. Gary Romenesko, Lari DeBruin, Ed Hammen, and the other teachers at St. John's Catholic Grade School—thanks for a foundation that shows that the Gospel and social action go hand in hand. Tony Campolo for showing me passion, intellect, and love. We disagree on issues since this book was first written, but you still make me want to change the world. Tim Landis and Harry Thomas for taking a risk in me and for all your encouragement. Let's keep dreaming together.

Don and Dave Wilkerson for seeing addicts as people through the eyes of grace. Teens Encounter Christ for helping me fall in love with Jesus. Larry Crabb and Dan Allender for helping me apply grace to the pain of my story, enabling me to speak grace into other people's lives.

I'd also like to thank the people who have helped get my crazy thoughts down in print. Carla (Schmalz) Vandenheuvel for transcribing my messages. Lisa (Donner) Strom for your original work and challenge on Chapter Two. Mary Rockman for your input and help with Chapter Four, and for your life-long friendship as well as your 30-plus years at Life Promotions. Tammy Borden, a great assistant, for making sense of my scribbles even when I couldn't read them. For your hours and hours of dictation, for your ideas, editing, and helping me say what I'm trying to say. I couldn't have done this without all of you.

I want to thank Jeanne Juve, Mary Lenz, and Joyel Vandenboogart for their contribution to the updated edition of Grace. Thank you for your labor of love and time coordinating the edits, pictures, formatting, and all that was entailed with the new edition. This book is going to continue to reach more people because of your work. Thank you.

To Mitzi Lyon, Jonathan Kopecky, and Gary Bach, three youth leaders who have expanded this book with questions for small group leaders from their own youth groups. Thank you for allowing us to use some of your insight to create the study guide so that people can go deeper into grace and find more freedom. Thank you Lucas Tuttle for taking all of these questions and helping to put them into final form for the book.

To Jesus for interrupting my story with His grace.

TABLE OF CONTENTS

FOREWORD

It's been in the top five of favorite hymns for generations, and causes tears to well up in the eyes of saints and sinners alike when bagpipes wail it out at the funerals of fallen heroes. "Amazing Grace" was penned in 1779 by John Newton, a slave-ship captain, after he had a miraculous encounter with grace itself. He declared that it "saved a wretch" like him. Truth is, it has saved many a wretch—like me, and Bob Lenz, and anyone who has received it as the gift it is from the nail-scarred hands of Jesus.

How is it possible that the greatest gift that can be given—salvation—can only be received by this thing called grace? As Bob makes so abundantly clear in this book, no amount of work or effort can earn it. Nothing we could ever do could make us worthy enough to deserve it. It is a gift to every one of us in our wretchedness—grace that is amazing, indeed.

Not only is grace the foundation of our salvation in Christ, it forms the very essence of our day-to-day lives as His followers. Who we are, what we do, and the purpose of life itself is all bound up in grace. We have worth not because of what we own or what we have achieved. We have worth *only* because of Who gives us worth—our Creator, by His grace. He lovingly knit us in our mother's womb (Psalm 139). He took delight in creating our personalities, beauty, talents. He carefully etched our unique fingerprints, designed the way we laugh, implanted what will make us cry—from both joy and sorrow. We are truly "fearfully and wonderfully made." As each child is born, I'm convinced God looks at His handiwork and says, as He did at Creation, "Oh, that's good. That's very good!" And then for all our lives, nothing we could ever do would make Him love us more. And nothing we could ever do would make Him love us less, either! What enormous loads could be lifted off our backs if we could only grasp this, believe it, and receive it for what it is—our loving and merciful God's grace.

But then comes the tricky part. Having received our salvation by grace and having been formed in grace, we are now expected to give grace to all around us. We were not made to be buckets that merely receive grace and then, with grateful hearts, store it safely, careful not to spill a drop. No, we are expected to be pipes through which grace freely flows. We receive it so that it can flow through us to bless others. And this is another amazing thing about grace—the more we give it away, the more of it we receive, flowing into us and then through us.

A great tragedy across the world is that many who have yet to receive God's grace for salvation watch very carefully those of us who have, and too often we look like stagnant buckets—smug, self-righteous, judgmental and unloving. The world has clearly gotten the message about what we are against, but too seldom hears about what we are for. So little grace trickles out of our pipes that people feel judged, unloved, devalued and rejected by us. And many assume they must be viewed the same way by the Lord we represent. But of course that's not true. They are loved desperately by the Source and Giver of Grace, God Himself. Jesus lived a life full of grace. He got in lots of trouble with the religious authorities of His day (buckets) for how He graciously treated those deemed to be worthless by their man-made, rule-bound measures. Jesus loved nothing more than to extend grace to the outcasts, the poor and oppressed all around Him. The question for us is: Who are those people in our lives and in the world today? We don't need our WWJD bracelets for this one, because we already have the example of WDJD—What Did Jesus Do? And what does He therefore also expect of us?

The best way to understand grace is not to dissect it, analyze it and pontificate about it—it is better caught than taught. That's why I love this book Bob has written. Bob is graceful—as in, grace-full! I have watched this gentle giant happily allow poverty-stricken children to gleefully use him as a jungle gym. I have witnessed him gracefully lead a peasant woman dying of AIDS to give her life, heart and future to Jesus. I've seen that same spirit stir the hearts of tens of thousands of young people from the stage at a festival. I've fought tears as he gently ministered to both powerful leaders and defeated ministers around a campfire. He is a pipe through which grace gushes!

This book allows you to do what I've done for a couple of decades—hitch a ride with this remarkable man. He is desperate for you to truly understand the life-changing wonder of God's amazing grace. Listen to his stories, laugh at his jokes, feel his heart, weep with him, share his outrage and his compassion. Then join his cause, allowing God's grace to not only flow into you, but through you, too. Amazing grace—there is no "sweeter sound" to our hearts, no higher calling for our lives.

Dr. Wess Stafford
President Emeritus
Compassion International

INTRODUCTION

A book about grace. I've been afraid to write it for fear it wouldn't measure up. Ironic, huh? Grace is the title and measure up is in the subtitle. Although this book may never match books on grace that have impacted me, I believe this book will give you the power to be the person God intended you to be.

Because I have met so many people who have not experienced God's grace, this book is for you. Or maybe you're one of those who have experienced grace, but don't live in it. I encourage you to jump back into His arms.

Or maybe you're among those who think, "I've now turned my life around and no longer need grace to live," thinking it was necessary only for the beginning of your Christian walk. Together, let's see our daily need for Jesus and His grace and return to our first love.

ONLY GRACE

Grace is the only theology that works,
the power that sets my heart free,
the only voice that silences the lies of insecurity.

Grace is the only thing that takes away my guilt
and shame,
the only mirror that allows me to feel beautiful as a
child of God.

Grace is the only thing that helps me get back
up when I fall,
the only freedom that allows me to dream,
the only agent to help me believe there is something better
and that I can live better because of it.

Grace gives me confidence to know I can make a
difference in this world.

It's the only thing that helps me believe that His
Kingdom can come,
and His will shall be done on Earth as it is in Heaven.

Grace is the only medicine that heals my hurt
and heart,
the only thing that helps me not judge or
alienate others,
and the only thing that tames my ego.

Grace is the only hope for my marriage, my kids, my friendships, my faith, my church.

It is the only hope for our world.

Grace. God offers it to all—to those who feel as if they don't measure up and even those of us who think we do.

THE FREE GIFT 1

I love Christmas! It is one of my favorite times of the year. From the gifts, to the lights and decorations, the family gatherings and gifts, the mistletoe, eggnog, garland and gifts, the surprises, smiles, hugs and gifts, the flash of the camera, music and…did I mention gifts?

I love Christmas more than ever since my wife, Carol, and I now have five children. They have made it fun for me again. Seeing their joy and anticipation for Christmas morning is contagiously exciting, and I love seeing them open their gifts. It helps me vividly recall the joy of Christmas morning from my own childhood. Because of this, I've now come to enjoy the pleasure of giving gifts more than receiving. And as my children grow, I can see a desire growing in them to give gifts rather than receive them, as well. It warms my heart.

But to be truthful, another reason Christmas is thrilling for me again is because I get to play with my children's toys! The millennium has brought with it some fun stuff. From remote control vehicles, the latest iPhone, Xbox, PlayStation or Wii, to multiplayer computer games—these toys are awesome!

How do you know when you're getting old? For me, it was when I started getting underwear for Christmas…and I liked it. That's when it happened. You should see me open the carefully wrapped package with anticipation. I tear off the ribbons and paper, and I can't help but exclaim, "Oh! Fruit of the Loom! Oh Honey, and they're boxers too—not tighty whiteys like my dad wore! Cool! Thanks, Carol!"

I really like everything about Christmas. I love making Christmas cookies and Christmas candy. Wait. I should be honest. After all, this is supposed to be a Christian book. I love *eating* Christmas cookies and candy. I love picking out our tree as a family too. This year we even cut the tree down ourselves. You can be sure that next time I'm going to use a chain saw.

A few years ago, Carol and our three oldest children, Amber, Danielle, and David, were going to leave the day after Christmas for a mission trip. Everything seemed rushed. The normal hustle and bustle of the season was made even more intense because of all the planning for the trip. It seemed as if there was not enough time to get it all done.

THE TREE

To help out, I decided to pick up a Christmas tree on the way home from the office. I saw a sign at the tree lot—*ALL TREES $10*. Wow. *All* those trees for just ten bucks! So I started putting *all* the trees in my van. The guy selling the trees, or as he liked to refer to himself, the Tree Sales Associate, quickly clarified that it was any *one* tree for $10. What can I say? With my mom being Dutch, she taught me to always get my money's worth. So the next best thing was to pick out the biggest tree.

We own a conversion van so our family of eight, including my sister Lois, can go along when I travel to speaking engagements. Strapping the tree to the top of the van was quite a challenge. The tree hung over the front and the back of our van, plus over the edges on both sides. The sight resembled the Grinch's sleigh after he plundered Whoville. After the tree was finally secure, I headed home. Yes, the tree was a great deal. There was only one problem...*my wife wanted it in the house.*

Have you ever seen Christmas trees being transported from tree farms on a semitrailer truck? They're wrapped really small and tightly squeezed into a wire mesh. I never knew how they did that. Now I know… they pull them through my front door! Getting that tree through our door took all the ingenuity I could muster. Once it finally scraped through the doorframe, it sprung open in retaliation, knocking over everything in its path—showing no mercy.

Needless to say, the tree was too tall, even for our older two-story home. I can't even reach the ceiling in our living room, and I'm six foot four inches tall. First I cut off the top of the tree. It didn't fit. Second, I cut off some of the bottom of the tree. Still no go. After honing my skills as a lumberjack for an hour in my living room, it finally fit. Exhausted, I proudly propped the tree up and secured it in its base. It covered half of our living room and crowded out much of the furniture. It could no longer be called a Christmas tree. It was a Christmas bush.

Later I realized why it was so cheap. I think it was a tree left over from the year before. Did you ever have a tree like that? You simply walk in the room and needles drop to the floor. I warned the kids to be careful around the tree. Bad idea—especially with boys. They no longer casually walked into the room as they had a thousand times before. No. They suddenly felt inspired to stomp their feet as they walked through the room, then stand by the tree and jump up and down. Our tree was no longer green. Our floor was.

CHRISTMAS SONGS

I also love to go Christmas caroling. When the kids were young I loved taking them along. They would sing at the top of their lungs, making up lyrics when they couldn't remember the words. We would all join in as we went from one friend's home to the next. To be honest, I didn't take them along just because I was trying to be a good dad—when the kids were along, the grandmas and grandpas of the neighborhood would always give us more Christmas cookies and candy.

There's a Christmas carol that almost everyone knows by heart. Go ahead. Let the melody spring up inside you. And if you're brave enough, sing it out loud. Yes, even if you're reading this book in July. Here it goes…

Oh, you better watch out,
You better not cry.
Better not pout, I'm telling you why—Santa Claus is coming to town.
He's making a list,
He's checking it twice.

He's gonna find out who's naughty or nice.
Santa Claus is coming to town.
He sees you when you're sleeping,
He knows when you're awake.
He knows if you've been bad or good,
So be good for goodness' sake.
Oh, you better watch out.
You better not cry.
Better not pout, I'm telling you why—Santa Claus is
coming to town.[1]

Every audience I've asked to sing that song sings it without missing a word, and without lyric sheets or PowerPoint help. I suggest there is a philosophy in that song that goes something like this:

There's this guy who lives at the North Pole, wears red, and he's bigger than Bob. His name is Santa Claus. He's a powerful, super-intelligent, influential, one-of-a-kind, loaded rich guy. His actions depend on yours, and he's got his eye on you. So, you'd better behave, because he checks his list twice. He doesn't miss a thing. Oh, you may hide things from your mom and dad, but Santa will find you out, because he's even watching you when you're sleeping. There's no faking him. You can't get away with anything. He knew those pillows under your blankets weren't really you. He knows you weren't really sick when you faked it to get out of taking that math test in school. And here's the key. It all boils down to this: Santa knows who's naughty or nice, bad or good, and he's coming. Bottom line: you want him on your side.

The philosophy is clear. If you're good enough, you get gifts. If you're not good enough, you don't get gifts. If the latter is the case, you may have sung this song at Christmas time:

I'm getting nothing for Christmas.
Mommy and Daddy are mad.
I'm getting nothing for Christmas…"Why?"
'Cause I ain't been nothing but bad.
I put a tack on teacher's chair,
Somebody snitched on me.
I put some gum in my sister's hair,
Somebody snitched on me….[2]

Can you relate? I thought about this philosophy a little more. If you're good, you get gifts. If you're bad, you get no gifts. But if you have to do something to get a gift, it's not really a gift—it's a paycheck.

GIFT OR PAYCHECK?

For example, you work at your job for 40-50 hours, and at the end of the week your boss hands you a check. As you reach for your paycheck he says, "Here you go. Here's your gift." Now, I don't know about you, but my blood pressure would rise, and my face would turn red in anger. My jaw would lock, and I'd stand a few inches taller. I'd say through my clenched teeth, with my finger pointing in accusation, "What do you mean, a gift? I worked hard for this pay. I put my time in for this. I deserve this. I earned this!" If you work for something, it's not a gift. It's a paycheck. May I repeat myself? If you have to work for something, it's not a gift. It's a paycheck!

> **If you have to work for something, it's not a gift. It's a paycheck!**

Yet the words of that song and the meaning of that concept are burned into our minds and our psychological hard drives. The same applies to our society. If you're good enough, if you're pretty enough, if you're strong enough, rich enough, popular enough, productive enough, handsome enough, intelligent enough, talented enough, creative enough, athletic enough, thin enough, musical enough, nice enough…. If you have the right things in life, then you're someone. Then you'll earn acceptance. Then you'll go places and be somebody.

If not? If you don't measure up, then many times society will reward you with rejection and leave you feeling empty. Your tree in life will be left bare, with nothing beneath, despite all your efforts.

This philosophy causes many people to feel worthless and desperate. Feelings of defeat and constant failure flood their thoughts, and they struggle to find their purpose in life. They can't imagine facing another day of trying, only to feel emptier than the day before. Millions try to earn a reward of love, friendship, and value by striving to make it on the treadmill of life. Their lives are spinning out of control, and despite all their energy, ambition, and drive, it's never quite "enough."

STICKS AND STONES

Paul is a good example. When Paul was in elementary school he wasn't very tall. Instead, he was rather wide. His body would not always cooperate the way he wanted it to. Does the phrase "two left feet" ring a bell? In a school that elevated athletics and appearance, Paul was always picked last for gym class games, if picked at all. It hurt enough to be left out. When he finally was noticed, it was only to be laughed at, teased, or mocked. Paul had low grades, and the help from tutors added to the name-calling. We all know how cruel some kids can be.

Paul concealed his size by wearing solid, dark clothes, and a baggy, untucked shirt to hide how big he was. (Hmmm, I just described what I'm wearing as I write this. And it's not like I'm fooling anyone! It's not as though I stand up in front of a school and the crowd thinks, "Hey, look at the skinny guy with a microphone.")

Sixth graders were required to take showers in gym class. How could Paul possibly hide himself if he had to be naked in front of the other guys? Paul started getting sick on the days he had gym class. Was he really sick? No. He wanted to avoid the pain and humiliation of being completely exposed.

Paul's self-worth plummeted like a stock market crash, and his perception of his personal value was bankrupt. Feelings of worthlessness consumed his thoughts, and he desperately wanted the pain to go away. The next year a girl in his class committed suicide; her picture was right next to his in the yearbook. Paul contemplated what she had done, and thought that maybe ending his life would be the answer to his life of despair.

Paul told me that the day came when the pain of his rejection was so unbearable that he placed a noose around his neck and was ready to take his own life. Then he heard, "Paul, I love you. And no matter what anyone else may say, you are loved—not because of what you look like or what you can do, but just for who you are. Paul, you are loved." Because of those simple words, spoken years before by his mom, he couldn't go through with it.

Though Paul was big on the outside, for years he felt very small and insignificant on the inside because of the ridicule of his classmates. Until high school…

In high school, things started to change for Paul. He shot up to six foot two inches tall, and the only thing wide was his chest. He joined the football team. Girls noticed him—not only for his build, but also for his deep, golden bronze tan. His hair was brown, streaked with natural blonde highlights, and his baby blue eyes could win over any heart and weaken the knees. After learning he had a form of dyslexia and how to deal with it, Paul raised his grades to As and Bs. Guys would invite him to parties and girls would ask him to come over and study for "health" class…if you know what I mean.

ALL GOD'S CHILDREN

How sad that the different ways he was treated in elementary school and in high school were based totally on his outward appearance. The same guy they made fun of, laughed at, put down, and pushed to the brink of suicide—they later accepted solely because he slimmed down and had a good tan? Now he's good enough? Now he has the right stuff on the outside—the right kind of body, looks, and ability?

Passion burns in my soul and I want to scream so that all can hear me. Paul deserved no less respect when he was shorter and unpopular than he did as a popular football jock. He's the same person today as he was then. He's the same person on the inside as he was back then. The only thing that changed was the outside. His life is of no less or no greater value now than it was in sixth grade. Paul is my long-time friend, and I loved him just as much in elementary school and in high school as I do today, and it still brings me to tears to think I almost lost him because of what people value on the outside. I wonder, how many people like Paul have we lost?

FRIENDSHIPS

I get angry with the mind-set of most of today's society. I wish we could see others as God sees them—as the whole and beautiful person He created. Western culture dictates that if you're not good enough, you don't get the gift of friendship. Friendship is a gift, and if you have to work for it, then it's no longer a gift. It's a paycheck.

The "Santa Claus Is Coming to Town" philosophy has permeated our society. And sadly it has filtered its way into the church. If you're good enough, you go to Heaven. And if you're bad, you go to hell. As a child, I remember singing, "One, two, three, four, five, six, seven. All good children go to Heaven. When they get there they will say, my brother went the other way."

We may joke about it, but have you considered that maybe there really is a hell? It would sure ruin your day if you found out that you had to go there. As a matter of fact, it would ruin your eternity. I don't want to tell you this, and quite honestly, I wish I didn't believe this. But because I do, I must tell you. I believe in a real hell.

The more I read the Scriptures, the more convinced I am that there is a place where there is a separation from God and all that is good. (See Matthew 10:28, Luke 16:23, and Second Peter 2:4.) Once there, you can't get away, and you'll never experience the presence of God again. For those already in despair, it's hard to imagine an existence worse than the hell they already live in, and that's why suicide seems so appealing to so many.

There was a rock group I listened to in high school called AC/DC. One of their songs is "Highway to Hell," and a portion of it goes like this:

Don't need reason, don't need rhyme,
Ain't nothing I would rather do.
Going down, party time,
My friends are gonna be there too.
I'm on the highway to hell.[3]

Let me tell you, one thing I know for sure, one thing I can promise you—there will be no friendships in hell. If hell is the absence of God, and the Bible makes it clear that God is love (see 1 John 4:7-8), then there will be no love in hell. No relationships. No friendships. So please, please don't go there for a friend, or think that you will find a friend. Within God is where friendships and love are found, where relationships flourish, where eternal life exists. Eternity in Heaven will be full of love and acceptance and friendships.

ALTAR FALTER

A lesson from my own life demonstrates the good=Heaven and bad=hell philosophy. Growing up Catholic, nuns made an impact on my life.

As a boy, the nuns taught me about God's goodness, but they also taught me about the law—and

I am forever grateful. They taught me that there is a right and a wrong, that you reap what you sow. They also taught that there are a lot more *Thou shalt not's* to obey than are listed in the original Ten Commandments. I was very involved in the church. I was even an altar boy. It was great! I was even the *head* altar boy, and I got to light the candles. It was a big responsibility, for we had a large parish.

There must have been over 700 people at mass that day. It was my first time, and I was being watched by the nun in charge, Sister Louisiana. She made me look small. Our altar had a door on either side, and she was standing off to the left making sure that I correctly performed my altar boy duties. I had to remember where to bow and where to genuflect, or kneel, out of respect. I thought I was doing a great job. I lit all the candles. Now all that remained was the final task. I was supposed to extinguish the flame at the tip by pulling the little lever and the wick would retract inside, extinguishing the flame. But there I stood, not knowing what to do. I panicked. I was afraid. I think it was "altar fright."

I decided to do what any fast-thinking, responsible altar boy would do—blow it out. So, I tried to casually blow on the flame in hopes that no one would see. But apparently I didn't know my own strength, for as I blew, the wick broke off and the flame fell to the floor and caught the carpet on fire. In a calm, cool, and collected altar boy fashion, I screamed, "Ah! Ah! Ah!" As I saw the flame flickering beneath me, I frantically stamped out the fire, pounding my feet into the floor as I yelled. Looking back, I'm surprised I didn't stop, drop, and roll.

The entire congregation watched, but their moment of wide-eyed concern quickly turned to laughter, everyone except Sister Louisiana. She was in the entrance of the left door. I ran toward the one on the right. Once I started to run, I became even more afraid, for as I looked back I saw Sister Louisiana sprinting across the altar toward me. You may think it's funny, but she didn't even genuflect as she passed the crucifix on her way to capture the little arsonist! Have you ever been chased by a nun? It's like a holy strobe light…black, white, black, white, black…. All I could think was, *I'm dead. I started God's house on fire! I'm going directly to hell. Do not pass go. Do not collect $200.*

For some time after that I thought I was going to hell. Then I met a priest, one of the greatest men I've ever met. His name was Father Papowski. I met him on a Teens Encounter Christ (T.E.C.) weekend. He told me, "Bob, you're not good enough to go to Heaven." I replied, "I know. That's what my mom says." He said, "No, Bob, you don't understand. Nobody's good enough on their own effort or works to go to Heaven. Not even me."

A FATHER'S LOVE

Not even him? I kept thinking, *This guy's a priest!* I knew what it took to be a priest: the dedication, the commitment, and the sacrifice. To be a priest meant you had to go to school forever and then promise to never get married, and that meant you'd never... wow. I thought this guy deserved to go to Heaven! But he told me, "No, Bob. The Bible makes it clear in Romans 3:23 that *all* have sinned and fall short of the glory of God." The Scripture kept reeling in my mind. OK. Everybody sins. But isn't God keeping tabs? Isn't He keeping a checklist? And if you have more good things than bad when you die, you're in. Right?

But then I read Romans 6:23: "The wages of sin is death." See, you get paid for being bad. It's the paycheck for sin and breaking the law; it's the paycheck for breaking God's moral code. Just like Father Papowski said; we have all sinned, and we all deserve eternal death. We have all earned a place in hell.

I assumed the verse would continue on in its natural progression. I thought, *If being bad **earns** eternal death, then the rest of the verse is going to tell me how* *being good will **earn** eternal life.* Right? I thought it would show that the paycheck for living right is to live forever.

If this were true, then the philosophy of Santa Claus rewarding only the good would be biblical. But it isn't true, and the verse doesn't end that way. It says, "the wages of sin is death, but the *gift* of God is eternal life in Christ Jesus."

Think of it like this:

You can work your way to hell or you can receive a free gift of eternal life.

It's free.

That's why it's the Good News—the Gospel.

It is a gift.

You can't earn your way into Heaven.

If you have to work for something,

it's not a gift.

It's a paycheck.

God's love and His salvation are free gifts,

not based on merit,

but on His tender mercy and grace.

GRACE

Grace. I'll never forget the first time I got a taste of it. It was Christmas morning and I was in the fourth grade. It had been a tough year as far as my behavior was concerned. I was a rambunctious boy with unending energy. I had caused some trouble at school, which prompted calls from the nuns to my parents. I was in trouble at home, too, for not helping around the house as much as I was expected to. I got in trouble in the neighborhood too, even though I insisted nothing was ever my fault. You could always hear me spouting excuses like, "He started it," or "I didn't break the window; the ball did!"

My dad told me on Christmas Eve that I wasn't getting anything for Christmas. He said, "Bob, you have to learn your lesson. You can't keep behaving like this. All your choices have consequences." I protested in response, "Come on, Dad!" But he replied, "No. Bob, you don't *deserve* anything."

I went to bed thinking to myself, *My dad doesn't lie. He's a man of his word. Maybe I'm not getting anything for Christmas.* I was sad as the reality of my consequences hit me. *He's probably right,* I thought. *I don't deserve anything, and he doesn't even know* **half** *of the things I've done.* Still, being a kid, I thought, *Maybe he did get me something after all…even if it's just something small.* I secretly hoped there would be something, anything, waiting for me under the tree, even though I knew my actions deserved no- thing. I fell asleep, unsure of what the morning would bring.

We don't deserve anything but we receive everything through His grace.

You know how kids are on Christmas morning. It's hard to get them out of bed for school, but when December 25 rolls around, they are up at 4:30 a.m. ready to race to the Christmas tree and start tearing open presents.

That Christmas morning was no different. I was the first one up. I walked anxiously, yet apprehensively, toward the living room, wondering, hoping, that maybe something small would be there for me despite my father's words the night before. But there wasn't something small.

As I turned the corner, I couldn't believe my eyes. There, right in front of the tree, bigger than life, was a brand-new bike. And it was for me! How could I tell? It had my name on it: BOB. Then I read it backward just to be sure: BOB. Sure enough, it was for me! It wasn't just an ordinary bike either; it was one of the custom deluxe bikes of the time. The scene felt surreal with the morning light streaming in from the window, shining against the bike's chrome handlebars and vinyl banana seat. It had a sissy bar and gold sparkles. I screamed and jumped up and down, unable to contain my excitement. I ran toward it, grasping the handlebars and jerking it from where it had been positioned so carefully the night before. I hopped on the seat and sat there with my mouth gaping open in disbelief. My hands stayed firmly clenched on the handlebars, imagining it was a dream, knowing it was not.

I remember being so proud and arrogant. I hopped off the bike and walked up to my dad and said, "Dad, I thought I didn't *deserve* anything." He looked at me with a look I'll never forget. He said something with such tenderness and compassion that it pierced straight through my heart. "Bob," he said, "you didn't. And you don't *deserve* anything. But I still love you."

I was speechless. Touched by his mercy, I had tasted grace. I had received a true gift, for I hadn't earned it. I didn't get what I deserved. I was loved unconditionally, not based on my performance or behavior, but on my father's goodness. Even as a fourth grader, my response wasn't, "Cool! It doesn't matter how I live." Not at all. I was humbled by his extravagant gift, remorseful for what I had done, and my heart was overwhelmed with gratitude for his goodness.

That's what the love of God is like. We don't deserve it. We can't earn it. We can't buy it. God has chosen to love us, not based on our goodness, but on His desire to love us through His ultimate Free Gift—Jesus.

ENDNOTES

1. "Santa Claus Is Coming to Town," lyrics by J. Fred Coots and Haven Gillespie, © 1934.

2. "I'm Getting Nuttin' for Christmas," lyrics by S. Tepper & R. Bennett, © 1955.

3. "Highway to Hell," lyrics by AC/DC Volume 1, © 1979. Written by Angus Young, Macolm-Young and Bon Scott.

CHAPTER 1 DISCUSSION QUESTIONS

1. Christians talk about grace a lot, but do we really know what it is? What is GRACE?

2. If you have to do something to receive a gift, is it really a gift? Do you consider your relationship with God more like a paycheck or a free gift?

3. Does your church make you feel like you need to work, volunteer, or do certain things in order to be a good Christian?

4. How did Paul's story end?

   • According to his classmates, what made him good enough?

   • According to Jesus, what made him good enough?

5. Do you believe that there is a hell? What do you imagine hell to be like?

6. Do you have anyone in your life that demonstrates grace? How have they shown it to you?

MOTHER TERESA DID NOT GO TO HEAVEN…

I've received a lot of heated reaction from this statement: Mother Teresa did not go to Heaven…. So much so, that I hesitated putting it in this book, much less making it a chapter title. I feared people might dismiss the whole book as extreme. There have been occasions as I've traveled around the country when I've spoken these words, and you can imagine the reaction. Mouths drop open in disgust. Eyes narrow in anger. People look at the person sitting next to them with that look that says, "What! Did I hear him right? How can he say that? Look at her life and all the wonderful things she did!"

But that is exactly my point. And that is why I have risked putting the statement in this book. But, I beg you to read on—there is an ellipsis at the end of the statement…those three dots. It means there's more. The phrase is incomplete. Read on. Don't stop now. Allow me to finish.

Mother Teresa did not go to Heaven…*because* of the good works she did.

I've never received flack when explaining about the free gift discussed in Chapter One. It seems that no one has a problem with explaining salvation from the angle of a loving father giving a gift to his fourth-grade son (who didn't deserve it) at Christmas. That seems to warm our hearts, and we quickly agree that God unconditionally loves us and is eagerly waiting to offer His salvation as a free gift, despite our miserable, sinful condition.

Yet, take that same truth and apply it to one of the heroes of our time. What happens when you apply the concept of grace to a person whom millions of people look up to as an icon of what it means to love and serve? Apply the concept of grace to Mother Teresa, someone whose lifestyle won and *earned* the respect, not just of Christians in and outside her own denomination, but also those from different world religions and non-Christians alike. It's a different story when you say that her life didn't guarantee her a place in Heaven.

Mother Teresa was an amazing woman. She set up orphanages, fed the poor, ministered to the imprisoned, and opened homes for those dying of AIDS. She also opened a facility for alcoholics, drug addicts, the homeless, and the destitute. She worked with those whom society had discarded and put aside as hopeless, including lepers. "I realize that when I touch the odorous and oozing members of a leper, I am touching the body of Christ..." said Mother Teresa.[1] Stories are told of how she helped a woman who was half eaten by rats. When most people would have turned in disgust, she knelt down to serve. She led a sacrificial life and inspired others to do similar good deeds. She truly displayed pure kindness and selfless humanitarianism.

SAVED THROUGH CHRIST

But if people could earn their way into Heaven because of good works, then we wouldn't need what Jesus did to save us from hell. If we could win a place in Heaven, we can save ourselves. Of course that is not possible. If our deeds save us, then Jesus' virgin birth, His sinless life, His being fully God and fully man, His passion and His resurrection, are not essential for our salvation. Why did Jesus have to suffer on the cross? If it is possible to avoid hell by how we live, then why the crucifixion?

Galatians 2:21 says it this way: "I do not set aside the grace of God, for if righteousness could be gained through the law, Christ died for nothing." The same verse from the New Living Translation says: "I do not treat the grace of God as meaningless. For if keeping the law could make us right with God, then there was no need for Christ to die."

If we could be saved by being a good person, then Jesus was not the Savior of the world, but merely our example. If being a good person is enough, then He is not the Lamb of God who takes away the sins of the world, but only a role model for how we should live.

If we could attain a place in Heaven based on our efforts, then the most famous of all Scripture references would read like this: For God so loved the world that He gave His one and only Son, that whoever would follow His example and try to be really good (as good as Mother Teresa) shall not perish but have eternal life.

But the Bible doesn't say that. It says, "For God so loved the world that he gave His one and only Son, that whoever *believes in Him* shall not perish but have eternal life" (John 3:16). Can it be any clearer?

This truth is carried out in Jesus' last words while He

was hanging on the cross. His final words to us were **not...**

Be good...*so you can make it to Heaven one day.*

Try hard...*just be committed and you can do it.*

Be positive...*believe in yourself.*

Do your best...*give it all you've got.*

He didn't even say...*WWJD...in all you do.*

So what *did* Jesus say? He said, "Father, forgive them. They don't know what they're doing!" (See Luke 23:34.) Even Jesus, while on the cross, knew and recognized that those crucifying Him didn't understand. He saw how they strove and tried and struggled to make it to Heaven on their own.

I think asking what Jesus would do regarding a moral situation is a very good thing to ask. But a friend of mine, Michael Bridges from the band Lost and Found, summed it up best when he answered the question, "What Would Jesus Do?" Michael said, "If you really wanted to do what Jesus did, you would be born of a virgin, live a sinless life, do acts of miracles, die on the cross for the sins of all humanity, three days later rise from the dead, ascend into Heaven, and then send the Holy Spirit. Go ahead and try."

Do we ask, "What would Jesus do for our salvation," as though it were a challenge for us to be enough like Jesus to attain it on our own? Only Jesus can do something for our salvation. We cannot attain salvation on our own.

The people gathered were convinced that the only way to get to Heaven was to follow the Ten Commandments. But they didn't know what they were doing. They didn't realize that they were being offered a better way—the only way. So they crucified the One who opposed their beliefs and theology. The very people who sinned against God by crucifying Jesus, needed the blood they demanded from Him for their forgiveness. So many failed to see that the death they were demanding of Jesus was the only way they could truly have life. They tried so hard to do what they thought was right. In the end, their efforts still led them to the cross.

> Do we ask, "What would Jesus do for our salvation," as though it were a challenge for us to be enough like Jesus to attain it on our own?

It's the same today. So many strive and believe that their effort will somehow earn eternal life. They reject the idea that there's another way—through

Jesus alone. Much like 2,000 years ago, many reject Jesus and His message of grace. But Jesus wants to lovingly scream, "You don't know what you're doing! You're headed in the wrong direction and don't even know it!"

Jesus longed to forgive those putting Him to death, and He longs to forgive each one of us. Look at the word *forgive. For-give.* The second syllable is give. Yes…a gift. Forgiveness cannot be earned or merited, only freely received.

Jesus also said, "Truly I tell you, today you will be with Me in paradise" (Luke 23:43). He said this to a thief, a criminal. This criminal was being put to death alongside Jesus as punishment for his crime. The true nature of his crime is left to the imagination. What did he steal? Did he vandalize someone's home? Was he violent? Was this his first offense, or just the first time he'd been caught? Whatever the details, it is clear that the people of his day felt that the way he lived his life merited death. Yet Jesus promised him paradise. In contrast, it would seem that the way Mother Teresa lived her life would surely have merited Heaven. But it is mercy and grace that opened Heaven to the thief, and it's only through Christ's death and resurrection that anyone is welcomed into God's loving arms.

But one of the most profound things Jesus said from

the cross was: "It is finished." This simple statement declared that no more needs to be done to please God. His demand for holiness, perfection, and the fulfillment of the law has been accomplished in Christ. Jesus is saying, "Stop trying. The work has been done. The price has been paid."

If obeying the Ten Commandments is our only requirement to gain eternal life, then why did Jesus have to take the nails in His hands and feet? Why did He have to be whipped until His flesh lay open? Why did He have to be stripped of His clothes while being mocked and laughed at, hit and spat upon? Why were the crown of thorns pushed into His brow? Why did He have to feel the pain of betrayal through a kiss? Why was He denied three times by one of His closest friends and forsaken and left alone to face the soldiers? Why did He have to hear the crowds choose Barnabas, a murderer, to be set free? Why did they demand the life of Jesus, an innocent man, and shout, "Crucify Him! Crucify Him!" Why?

If there were any other way possible to claim His own and purchase eternal life for us, Jesus would have done it. Do you think Jesus would have chosen to suffer like that if He knew there was another way to get the same end result? There was no other way. Jesus even asked His Father, "If there be any other way, let this cup be taken away" (see Luke 22:42). But the Father made it clear that no one would ever be justified by the works of the law. So Jesus willingly chose to die on the cross for you, for me, and for the world, because that was the only way He could save any of us.

I saw a Christmas card that I believe explains it best:

If our greatest need had been information,
God would have sent us an educator.
If our greatest need had been technology,
God would have sent us a scientist.
If our greatest need had been money,
God would have sent us an economist.
If our greatest need had been pleasure,
God would have sent us an entertainer.
But our greatest need was forgiveness,
so God sent us a Savior.[2]

Titus 3:5 says, "He saved us not because of righteous things we had done, but because of His mercy; He saved us through the washing of rebirth and renewal by the Holy Spirit…."

Let me be clear. **No one** by human effort, good

morals, personal sacrifice, dedicated service, acts of kindness, commitments made, money given, or even love shown, will go to Heaven because of these things.

Why is understanding this concept so important? Because according to a 2007 Barna Research study, 54 percent believe that "if a person is generally good, or does enough good things for others during their life, they will earn a place in Heaven."[3] That means that more than one out of two people feel their eternal destiny is based on their ability and actions. That is not true. It is a lie. And I want to expose this lie for what it really is—a matter of life and death.

> More than one out of two people feel their eternal destiny is based on their ability and actions. That is not true. It is a lie.

Acts 4:12 tells us that "Salvation is found in no one else, for there is no other name under Heaven given to mankind by which we must be saved." No one is good enough to earn Heaven. Not even Mother Teresa.

The only people who will be in Heaven are those who know they deserve hell. And the only people who will be in hell are those who think they can earn Heaven.

If you know you can't earn Heaven on your own, you are ready to receive the unmerited, unearned gift called grace.

> *For it is by grace you have been saved, through faith—and this is not from your-selves, it is the gift of God—not by works, so that no one can boast (Ephesians 2:8-9).*

Many believe that if they just obey the Ten Commandments, the law, they'll get into Heaven. We, as a society, have used the law as a measure of how good a person is. If someone keeps the majority of the Ten Commandments, we figure they're a pretty good person. But God's intent for the Ten Commandments was exactly the opposite. He didn't give us the law so we could prove how good we are. The law was given to show people how guilty we are (see Gal. 3:19). The law is not a measure of our accomplishments, but our failure. Mother Teresa did a lot of wonderful things and she probably accomplished more good in her lifetime than some entire nations have in centuries. But according to Ephesians 2:8-9, it was not her effort that gained her entrance into Heaven.

HEAVEN'S ONE AND ONLY GATE

Who is welcomed into Heaven? John 1:12 says, "Yet to all who received Him [Jesus], to those who believed in His name, He gave the right to become children of God." It's not what we have done. It's what He did over 2,000 years ago on the cross of Calvary. Jesus died, was buried, and three days later rose from the dead as predicted by Scripture for the forgiveness of our sins so we could have entrance into Heaven. Salvation is not because of our works, but because of His.

I personally believe that Mother Teresa went to Heaven, but not because of the life she lived. Rather, because she believed in Jesus and His life, death, and resurrection. She went to Heaven, not because of what she had done, but because of what Christ has done.

There is no other way, no other entrance, no other forgiveness, and no other salvation. Mother Teresa was loved by God unconditionally, accepted eternally, and forgiven completely. She lived her life to express that Gospel to the world. She didn't do it to gain her salvation. She did it *because* of her salvation. She expressed her love for Jesus by loving others. In Matthew 25:40, Jesus said, "Whatever you do for one of the least of these brothers and sisters of mine, you do for me." Mother Teresa often served "the least of these" and she made a positive impact on the world.

Mother Teresa said, "Jesus is my God; Jesus is my

spouse; Jesus is my life; Jesus is my only love; Jesus is my all in all; Jesus is my everything. Because of this I am never afraid."[4]

HELPING OTHERS

Sometimes I wish it were possible to earn Heaven. Then I could challenge people concerning social ills and use it as motivation to be good and fuel their good works to improve society.

For example, I work with Compassion International, a nonprofit child advocacy organization dedicated to releasing children from poverty in Jesus' name worldwide.[5] I know and trust their work with children. They provide food and an education to help break the cycle of poverty in families and communities. They help provide medical needs and training for children's health issues. They also share the love of Jesus one-on-one with children from 26 countries. Sponsors build relationships with children through letters and pictures. You really can change the world, one child at a time.

Mother Teresa said, "If our poor die of hunger, it's not because God does not care for them. Rather, it is because neither you nor I are generous enough. It's because we are not instruments of love in the hands of God."[6]

I believe this with all my heart, and I challenge you to pray and consider sponsoring a child. I sincerely desire every child to be sponsored, for I have been to places where children are turned away from a meal because they only had enough to feed the children who were sponsored. It's that real.

Still, I wish I could add this statement: "If you sponsor a child, your chances of going to Heaven are fifty percent better. If you sponsor two children, you're in! Guaranteed. Three, you can take someone with you." It certainly would be an incentive to be generous, wouldn't it? It could be pitched as, "Help children and earn Heaven."

But I can't say that because it isn't true. Jesus is the only way, truth, and life. He is not merely *one* other way, among many. You can't simply decide which way works for you—Jesus for eternal life, or sponsoring a child. Take your pick. Then why sponsor a child, if not for salvation? Because of these words, "Thy kingdom come, Thy will be done, on earth, as it is in Heaven." Sponsor a child not to gain Heaven, but to spread a taste of Heaven on earth; to share Heaven with someone the same way that you experienced it…as a gift.

Jesus *is* the way, the truth, and the life. No one, including Mother Teresa, you, or me, comes to the Father except through Him. Period. (See John 14:6.) It's not politically correct to say that. It's not popular. It's not widely accepted. And people often discount that fact about Jesus as extreme. But not believing the truth doesn't mean it isn't true. Someone may label others as narrow-minded who believe what the Bible says. So I ask, "If someone is labeled as narrow-minded, does it mean they're wrong?" No. Truth is truth. It's God's word, and God doesn't lie.

There is a difference between wanting to emulate Jesus and being religious. Jesus has something to say about religious people. In biblical times, there were religious people called Pharisees who dedicated their lives to studying the Bible and living it down to the smallest detail, including caring for the poor. They were pillars of society and highly respected. Jesus even said, "Unless your righteousness surpasses that of the Pharisees and teachers of the law, you will certainly not enter the kingdom of Heaven." And I could add: Unless your righteousness surpasses that of Mother Teresa….

But being self-righteous is a sin and doing deeds only for recognition or for a "paycheck" won't gain God's approval. He holds no hoops to jump through. There's no quota of good deeds that needs to be filled. And there's no amount of human effort that will earn Heaven. Without Christ, we are all dead in our sin. Yes, even Mother Teresa, without Christ, would have spent eternity separated from God, despite all her wonderful works.

> *Then it would not be by grace, which is the one thing that separates Christianity from other world religions.*
> —*C.S. Lewis* [7]

You may sponsor a child, donate to the poor, or even save a person's life. But that will not earn you a place in Heaven. Only Jesus can do that.

Remember, Mother Teresa did not go to Heaven because of her good works...she went to Heaven because of the salvation provided by Jesus Christ. Consider sharing the love of Jesus with others as Mother Teresa did.

> *The Law came in so that the transgression would increase; but where sin increased, **grace abounded all the more,** so that, as sin reigned in death, even so **grace would reign through righteousness** to eternal life through Jesus Christ our Lord (Romans 5:20-21 NASB).*

ENDNOTES

1. Mother Teresa, *Mother Teresa: In My Own Words* (Random House Value Publishing, 1997).

2. B.J. Morbitzer, "God Sent Us a Savior" (1976).

3. Barna By Topic-Beliefs: Heaven & Hell, Barna 2007) www.barna.org;http://www.barna.org /FlexPage. aspx?Page=Topic&TopicID=3.

4. Mother Teresa, *Mother Teresa: In My Own Words* (Random House Value Publishing, 1997).

5. Visit www.compassion.com to learn more. Your tax-deductible support connects a child with a loving, church-based program.

6. Mother Teresa, *Mother Teresa: In My Own Words* (Random House Value Publishing,1997).

7. C.S. Lewis, *Mere Christianity* (HarperOne New Ed. Edition, 2001).

CHAPTER 2 DISCUSSION QUESTIONS

1. Why is it so hard to admit that Mother Teresa didn't earn heaven based on the good works she had done?

2. Who do you know with "Mother Teresa" like qualities?

3. On page **38**, it says, "The only people who will be in heaven are those who know they deserve hell. And the only people who will be in hell are those who think they can earn Heaven." What do you think this means? Do you ever find yourself thinking you deserve heaven, especially when comparing yourself to others who aren't as decent as you?

4. Why is it impossible to go to heaven on your own good deeds?

5. If we can't earn heaven by being good, what is our motivation for being a good person?

6. Why do you think it is so hard for people to acknowledge that they are a sinner and deserving of hell?

7. Who is welcomed into heaven?

CHARITY

CHARITY CASE 3

In light of catastrophes including 9-11, Hurricane Katrina, and worldwide earthquakes and tsunamis, we have witnessed generous hearts of people willing to give their time, talent, and treasure to make a difference. I believe people love to give. Let's just look at some of the statistics from the United States:

- *Nearly 4 out of every 5 adults—83%—donate money to one or more nonprofit organizations.*

- *The average giving per person is $1,232 per year.*

- *Total giving reached an estimated $240.72 billion per year.*

- *Approximately 83.9 million adults volunteer, representing the equivalent of over 9 million full-time employees at a value of $239 billion.*[1]

There is true joy in giving. These figures may not include the mom who offers her time to chaperone her children's school field trip, the dad who helps with the Sunday school lesson, or the young person who stays after school to tutor a classmate. Giving gives people a sense of satisfaction—it feels good. When you give gifts, tithes, or time to an organization, a cause, or church, something inside of you comes alive. The key to feeling good is knowing you are making a real positive difference.

At my church there seems to be a constant need for Sunday school volunteers. Our church has a lot of families with lots of children. Some people would rather not volunteer, especially if they don't have any children, or if their children are grown. But some have stepped out and made a difference. They made a sacrifice, and before long they were hooked on being in the classroom and seeing a vision for what could really happen. They truly felt the reward of their charity.

> **Charity: Provision of help or relief to the poor; alms-giving; something given to help the needy; alms; benevolence or generosity toward others or toward humanity.**

For example, they knew they were making a difference when the little 9-year-old boy confided in them that he had, indeed, received Christ into his heart. Or the time when the single mother of a troubled teenager thanked them for helping their daughter realize what a relationship with Christ really meant, which began a journey of healing together.

On the other hand, spending years in a classroom without ever seeing results would be deflating. When you are fortunate enough to see the result of your work, the fruit of your labor, it is exhilarating and helps you press on and not give up. When you see good, positive results, there is a sense of joy.

It is true for me as well. I mentioned that I work with Compassion International and sponsor a child. My wife and I actually had the privilege of meeting our sponsored child. He looked just like he did in the picture on our sponsor packet. Do you know why? It was him! It's not a scam. When I met the little boy, I saw the fruits of my giving. He was so precious and I knew that my financial support helped him, not only physically with food and clothing, but with spiritual mentoring and training. In the midst of poverty I saw hope in his eyes, and I knew I was part of instilling that hope. From that moment on I became even more passionate about promoting the organization and its efforts because I saw the results firsthand. If I didn't believe that my support really made a difference in his life, I wouldn't do it. Knowing you've made a difference is the key. Yes, there truly is joy in giving.

FLIP SIDE

But what about the flip side of giving? How hard is it for you to be on the receiving end of charity? How do you feel when you have to rely on someone else? What is that gnawing feeling you get when you ask for help and admit you are in need of something you can't provide or supply on your own?

My son David is really smart. He got straight As in high school. He graduated from Crown College with a degree in Biblical Studies and has his Master's from Wheaton College. But there was a time when I did wonder about him. When David was quite young, I remember watching him as he tried to get dressed by himself one day. He was trying to put on his pants, with some obvious difficulty. First he placed one foot carefully through one hole while trying to keep his balance. Then he sat down on the floor while trying to get the other foot in the other hole. As he sat up he lost his grip and his pants fell to his ankles. He finally stood up and reached down once again to pull them up, but he just couldn't get them to stay up. I remember saying, "David, let me help." His response was defensive. "I can do it." He pulled them up once again only to have them fall to his ankles. I pleaded gently,

"David…." He said, "Dad, I said it before. I can do it myself. I'm big now. Leave me alone." He pulled them up. They fell down. Finally, after repeatedly resisting my offers, he reluctantly allowed me to help him. The problem was not his sincerity in trying. The problem was: It wasn't his pants he was struggling with. It was his shirt! He was trying to put his shirt on as if it were a pair of pants. He simply didn't understand the difference or have the full ability to do it himself yet, so he eventually relented to my offer of help out of desperation.

There's something difficult about asking for help—and receiving it. It's hard. You desperately want the results, but you think you don't need assistance. Where did my young son David learn that concept? I wondered how my son had already learned to crave independence. And then I remembered. It was that book…

I remember the story well. It told of a sinister duo—creatures from another time and place. They broke into the world of little children and began to instill new values, doctrine, theology, and ideas in their little heads. The duo seemed so unassuming, yet were cunning in their innocence. It was only a matter of time until children worldwide would look to them for inspiration. It was only a matter of time before my children succumbed to their powers. Why didn't I see it coming? How could I have been a party to their brainwashing? They easily succeeded in teaching their theology and doctrine. Now it was time for me to battle their power and influence over my child! Well, OK, I may be exaggerating the situation a little. It wasn't exactly a sinister duo.

Truth be told—it was Bert and Ernie. *Ernie & Bert Can, Can You?* That was the title of the little Sesame Street book with cardboard pages and toddler teeth marks on the corners. The entire book told kids that they could do it themselves. Picture Bert holding his toothbrush and smiling. "Time to brush your teeth. I can do it myself." As you flip the page you see Ernie at the kitchen table saying, "It's time to pour your milk. I can do it myself."[2]

Granted, we need to teach our children that they can brush their teeth and pour milk themselves. And hopefully you know that I'm only joking when I refer to the book's characters as sinister and cunning! But the philosophy of complete independence, supported by the media, literature, peers, and the culture, has become imbedded in us since early childhood. We don't want to rely on anyone or anything. After all, we're taught that anything's possible if we just put our mind to it.

ACCEPTING HELP

For instance, have you ever slipped and fallen? At first you feel dumb and clumsy, and your first instinct is to look around to see if anyone noticed. What do you do when someone does notice, and they approach you with concern to offer their hand? Chances are you will say, "No, thanks, I'm all right. I've got it. I can do it. No problem. I'm OK. Oh, it's no big deal. I can handle it. I don't need your help." It's as though accepting the aid of someone who's concerned would demonstrate our weakness.

It's more difficult for some people to ask for help than others. More often than not, people are determined and encouraged to handle it themselves. Why? I really believe the truth is that most people don't want to be seen as a charity case. We don't want to ask for help or seem weak.

Case in point: I was scheduled to speak to a group of youth in Upper Michigan. Our office had sent the person organizing the event a supply of posters and flyers, along with a biography that had my picture on it. Soon afterward our office received a call from the man hosting the event. The basic gist of the conversation went like this: "If Bob is going to speak to youth today, he can't wear those ugly glasses that he has on in the promotional photo." I was pretty offended until I found out he was an optometrist.

Even so, I was uneasy that he expressed such a harsh critique of my glasses. That is, of course, until he said that he wanted to give me a free eye exam and a free pair of glasses. I had to swallow my pride, accept help, and admit that I couldn't afford another more stylish pair of glasses. We have such a hard time when we are humbled by correction, or humbled by offered help. We don't like feelings of inadequacy or feelings of not being good enough.

Another case in point: During a trip to Paris, France, we saw many people begging, on the subway, on the street corners, all over the city. They held out their hands to us with dejected, sad, and down-trodden looks. Some were actually crying. At first I wondered, *Come on! You look able-bodied. Why can't you help yourself? You could get a job. You look like you are in better shape than I am. Get up and get a job. You can do it yourself.* Then I saw a man who was missing both legs. He had a little paper cup for donations, and my heart was moved. I thought, *Compare that to what we always said about Christianity; one beggar showing another beggar where to look for bread.*

We don't really want to be beggars, do we? We don't really want to be in that position of having our hand out. I'm not saying that all the beggars in France were legitimate. But even for those who weren't, I couldn't imagine what it took to have their self-pride, if you will, brought to a point where they would hold out their hands and say, "I need help." It can be degrading.

But unless we're willing to come to that same place with God, how will we ever receive? Do you go to God thinking you have what it takes,

> **Unless we humble ourselves and hold out our hands to God in total and helpless submission, we will never receive the love that He has for us.**

that you have the ability, the goodness, and the wherewithal to earn His love? Or are you in the place of a beggar, saying, "I can't do it myself"?

I don't like those feelings. I don't like to feel helpless, like a charity case; but that is what we need to be in front of our Lord.

> *Remember, dear brothers and sisters, that few of you were wise in the world's eyes or powerful or wealthy when God called you. Instead, God chose things the world considers foolish in order to shame those who think they are wise. And he chose things that are powerless to shame those who are powerful. God chose things despised by the world, things counted as nothing at all, and used them to bring to nothing what the*

world considers important. As a result, no one can ever boast in the presence of God (1 Corinthians 1:26-29 NLT).

God alone made it possible for you to be in Christ Jesus. He is the One who made us acceptable to God.

The verse in First Corinthians tells us that God chose the foolish, powerless, and despised; those who were counted as nothing at all. I don't want to be called foolish, powerless, despised, and nothing at all. I want to be important. I want to say that I did it, that I matter. But the funniest, most ironic thing is that when you are in the place of receiving charity from the Lord, you don't feel like a nothing. You feel like you matter. You feel the worth of God saying, "I love you!"

Let it be known that no one can ever boast in the presence of God. I think there are a lot of arrogant Christians, including me, boasting of their goodness, instead of saying, "It's only made possible to be in Christ because of what God has done. God alone. I'm a charity case."

Even our churches are reinforcing our independence and determinism. Many a sermon tries to pump up the congregation to give it all they've got. Don't give up. Don't give in. Do more. Give more money. Give more time. Take more classes. Try harder. Have more faith so you can get more blessings. Sadly, many preachers have turned their pulpits into platforms for motivational speeches rather than preaching the Gospel and the relevance of Scripture in their lives.

> If you're not a charity case, you're not a Christian!

The core message of this chapter is one that is unpopular in our culture. It's not fun to think about, and it's not fun to feel. It screams against everything inside of us. It gives us that uneasy feeling of help-lessness. It takes us off guard and goes against our human nature. If we say we're Christians, then we need to admit we're charity cases.

Most people love to give a helping hand and say, "Hey! Here you go." Yes, people love to give, but we hate being charity cases. God doesn't work that way! He wants us to be dependent on Him. He wants us to seek His love and will for our lives. When we are too independent, we think we've made it on our own. We take credit for what God has provided for us.

"I'LL NEVER BE A CHARITY CASE!"

The desire not to be a charity case runs deeply, indeed. Ronnie had called our hotline desperate for answers about how he could find a way to function and live without taking his prescribed medication. The medication was to treat a chemical imbalance. He had convinced himself that he shouldn't have to rely on it to make him better. We established a relationship and he came to the church for meetings.

He was determined to be strong enough to handle his life without the medication by doing it himself. I tried to convince him to let us help him and encouraged him to get professional help. I told him that we were blessed to have doctors who understood cases like his. But he didn't believe me. One time when he came in he was having a particularly hard time. He was crying and still searching for answers as to why he wasn't strong enough to handle things, and why he was failing to figure it out on his own. He couldn't understand why the harder he tried, the worse his life seemed to become.

I put my arm out to console him and placed my hand gently on his shoulder. "Ronnie," I urged, "let us help you. Let God and the doctors help you." I'll never forget his reaction. I've never seen anything like it.

His face became placid and his eyes intensified like fire. I could almost feel the adrenaline pumping through the bulging veins in his neck as his jaw clenched slightly. It was a look of determination. It reminded me of the look you'd want a football team to have when running out onto the field for the big game. It was a look that you would imagine seeing in the eyes of a man battling for his life on the front lines of war. Ronnie stood up. "No!" he screamed. "No! Never! I will never be a charity case!" He walked out of my office. My heart still breaks and grief still grips my heart, because the next time I saw him was at his funeral. Even though we had gone to great lengths to get him help through crisis intervention agencies and others, he took his own life. His determination to fight the battle of life himself ended up costing him his own.

Life is a process of giving and receiving. But we have conditioned ourselves, especially in this Western culture, to be strong, successful, to not rely on others, to not show weakness, and to be a man or a woman independent of others. Ronnie felt he even failed God because he just couldn't shake the depression and "just get over it" like so many Christians had encouraged him to do. Believe harder. Have more faith. Try harder. Read this. Do that.

He met the challenge head on and he had given it his all. He had given his car to a charity, sold all his possessions and gave the money to the poor. He tried harder to overcome his troubles than anyone I have ever met. He was determined to be a good person, to feel valuable and worthwhile. But his efforts left him empty.

Have you ever felt tired of trying and trying and trying? You've probably heard the phrase, "No man is an island." But just as equally you will hear people say, "I'm determined to be the last one standing," or "I'd rather die than go on welfare." What is this lie in society, this stubborn will that says, "Never say uncle? I'll never bow the knee or admit I'm broken. I don't need a power higher than myself. I don't need God and other people."

We do not have a God who twists our arm. Rather, He calls and beckons us, reaching out with a helping hand. Do we look Him in the face and scream, "No! Never! I can do it myself!" Or do we humbly say, "Yes, I'll receive the love You're offering." It brings humility, but love must be received. Michael W. Smith sings a great song called "Give It Away." It contains the line, *"Love isn't love until you give it away."* This is a true statement, but it is incomplete. Love isn't truly love until it is *received*. I may give you a gift, but unless you receive it, you will never enjoy or reap its benefits. It is the same with love. It can never be experienced until it is received.

RECEIVE

Life Promotions is a nonprofit organization that reaches youth around the world for Christ. A few years back while I was speaking at a conference for Life Promotions, a man walked up to me and my wife, Carol, and handed me a check made out to the ministry for $5,000! For a moment I didn't quite know how to react. A prideful response would have been to tell him that I didn't have to rely on someone else's donation to make a living, and that I didn't need his help because I could do it myself. Part of me was humbled, and I thought, *Gee, I must not be a very good speaker if I can't even make a living at it and have to ask people for help.*

But at that moment, my wife and I looked at each other and got choked up. We had tears in our eyes and looked in disbelief at the sacrifice that lay in my hand. I thought, *He believes in this. We are loved. We're believed in and he believes that God is going to use this ministry to reach people.* That's what it's supposed to feel like. But we're such a self-sufficient society that we have a hard time receiving.

Many people enjoy the experiences of mission trips. Often one of the requirements of going on a mission trip is to send a letter requesting financial support to friends and family. Some people have enough money to pay for their trips and don't need to send out support letters. Even so, I often encourage them to send a letter all the same. Their typical response is, "No, we don't want to ask for help."

When we take a mission trip to a developing country, go to an inner-city area, or travel to New Orleans to help those still recovering from Katrina, we expect those people to receive our help, don't we? We might even be offended if they didn't. But when we're asked to place ourselves in that same position of receiving help, we are often hesitant and unwilling to allow ourselves to receive help from others. It requires that we humble ourselves to receive assistance and say, "I need your help," whether it's money, prayer, or service.

The only people who will be in hell are those who refuse to receive. This is a bold statement, yet true. It's easy to give, but unless you receive and come to the point of confessing that you need what God has to offer, it will never be enough. We've got to come to the point when we realize we are needy, and receive what He is giving. Unless we receive Jesus Christ as our personal Savior, we are refusing God's greatest gift.

> *When we were utterly helpless, Christ came at just the right time and died for us sinners* (Romans 5:6 NLT).

Can you honestly bring yourself to that point of humility? Can you honestly say that you're utterly helpless and unable to attain Heaven on your own? Or do you still think you somehow play a role in redeeming yourself?

AT CHRIST'S EXPENSE

"I am not ashamed of the gospel…" (Rom. 1:16 NASB). This is a great verse, and pastors, priests, and preachers are quick to teach on it. They'll talk about the missionaries who endure persecution and the kids who aren't afraid to stand up for their faith in a public school. Stories are told of professional athletes and their boldness for Christ in the public arena. I think it's great to affirm those who are bold for the Gospel and I agree that we should all stand up for what we believe and not hold back.

But the next part of that verse is often disregarded as though a topic for a different sermon at a different time. I believe that the next part is the most important: "…for it is the power of God for salvation…."

It's the *power of God!* It's not the power of our boldness. It's not the power of our witness, and it's not the power of our unashamed stance for the Gospel. It is the power of God. What's the only thing that can save you and me? The Gospel. The gift. We can't save ourselves. When we think of the awesome power of God and His grace that saves humankind from our sins, we become excited about it and unashamedly proclaim it. When we truly think of what He has done for us, it is powerful! Because of His grace, we are saved.

There's a great definition for grace that is easy to remember:

G—God's
R—Riches
A—At
C—Christ's
E—Expense

We have a hard time receiving something at the expense of someone else, don't we? I'll never forget when my brother preached a message called *Divine Exchange*. "What a deal!" he said. "You bring your sinfulness; He gives you righteousness. You give Him what you've done wrong; He makes you perfect in God's sight." It's the divine exchange. You can't earn it. You don't deserve it. It's totally free. That's GRACE.

Somebody once told me, "Bob, if that's true, then why is it so hard for people to believe?" I think it's because people would rather hear a message that tells them they have to give it all they've got. People want to believe that they have what it takes and that they are capable, competent, and courageous enough to achieve anything despite the obstacles. It's been ingrained in our minds that if we simply apply ourselves and reach for our goals, then nothing is unattainable. You rarely hear anyone say that your "all-you-have" is not enough. We want to encourage and convince others, and ourselves, that as long as we do our best, that's what counts.

A friend of mine, Al, has four children. His youngest daughter, Callie, is adorable. A few years ago Al and his family were at our house for an Easter egg hunt. After the hunt some of the children were playing soccer, while others were jumping on the trampoline. Al and Callie were playing with a ball, throwing it back and forth. If one of them missed the ball they had to walk over to where it landed and pick it up. Al threw the ball a little too hard and Callie missed it. It went flying past her and rolled beneath the low, prickly branches of a pine tree. Knowing that his daughter could get scratched, Al asked her if she needed some help.

She said in that cute little 4-year-old voice, "No, Daddy, I can do it." She crouched down to take on the coniferous beast face first! Al and I quickly grabbed the branches and pulled them back for her. Almost unaware of our presence, she simply scooted in without ever touching a branch, grabbed the ball, and said, "See, Daddy. Look, I told you I could do it myself." She hadn't even noticed what we had done to help her. She thought she had done it all on her own, even though her father and I were the ones who made it possible.

So often this same principle applies to our lives. We plow forward, convinced we're the ones who have made the accomplishments and strides in our own lives, and we don't take time to become aware of the role the Father has had in making all things possible. We may not be so prideful that we think we are responsible for our own salvation; but what about that good grade, or that promotion? Do we give God the credit for all the good things that happen in our lives? He is the God who loves to give gifts to His children. All we have to do is receive them.

I heard about a guy who was walking along and saw a turtle stuck on top of a fence post. He imagined all the scenarios of how it could have gotten there. But one thing he knew for sure, it didn't get there without help.

Salvation may seem easy because it is free to us through the grace of God. But there was a price that was paid. Christ shed His blood, and the only way there is forgiveness is in the shedding of blood.

Second Corinthians 12:9 says, "…My grace is sufficient for you, for My power is made perfect in weakness…." Paul goes on to say, "Therefore I will boast all the more gladly about my weaknesses…."

When is the last time you went to church and heard people boasting about their weaknesses? I have a hard time admitting my weaknesses, much less going around boasting about them. But Paul clearly knew that the only entrance to salvation and knowing more of Jesus was through admitting

We can't go beyond our limitations without help.

his need. Most people only go to the doctor when they are sick. Likewise, if we don't realize we're sick, or sinful, then we'll never go to God. We can't do it on our own.

Another acronym to remember is the following for pride:

P—*People*
R—*Relying*
I—*In*
D—*Doing*
E—*Enough*

Pride is the ugliest thing. In *Rediscovering Holiness* by J.I. Packer, the issue of pride is addressed in its relation to grace. It is a great book, and I recommend it. From the title you may assume it focuses on doing more things to become more holy or Christ-like. I picked up this book because I had been writing and reading so much on grace that I wanted a change of pace. But I was surprised when I discovered that his book on holiness was entirely focused on grace. J.I. Packer, one of the best theologians of our time, reinforced that grace was at the center of holiness. Here's an excerpt:

> *Healthy souls…Only through constant and deepening repentance can we sinners maintain our souls in health. Spiritual health, like bodily health, is God's gift. But, like bodily health, it is a gift that must be carefully cherished, for careless habits can squander it. By the time we wake up to the fact that we have lost it, it may be too late to do much about it. The focus of health in the soul is humility, while the root of inward corruption is pride [People relying in doing enough]. In the spiritual life, nothing stands still. If we are not constantly growing downward into humility, we shall be steadily swelling up and running to seed under the influence of pride. Humility rests on self-knowledge; pride*

reflects self-ignorance. Humility expresses itself in self-distrust and conscious dependence on God; pride is self-confident and, though it may go through the motions of humility with some skill (for pride is a great actor), it is self-important, opinionated, tyrannical [meaning dictatorship], pushy and self-willed.4

Pride goes before destruction, a haughty spirit before a fall (Proverbs 16:18).

God is calling His people to be humble. It's the entrance into salvation, and it's the key to walking daily with Jesus. No matter how good a person you are, you still need to admit your need for God. The proudest people I know are also the most insecure. That's why they have to live a life of image, appearance, and performance.

> **The proudest people I know are the most insecure.**

CHARITY CASES

I tried to make this point one day when I was speaking at a church's Sunday morning service. There was a young girl in the front row who helped me illustrate it well. As I approached, her eyes grew big. Her name was Morgan and she was 12 years of age. After brief introductions I asked her, "Did you ever hear that Jesus loves you so much that if you were the only person left on earth, He still would have died just for you? He loves you that much."

She smiled approvingly.

"Morgan, you're twelve years old, right?"

She nodded.

"Have you ever gotten drunk?" I asked.

She rolled her eyes, shook her head, and said, "No."

Some soft gasps and nervous giggles echoed throughout the sanctuary.

I continued. "Morgan, did you ever do drugs like marijuana?"

Once again she emphatically denied it.

"Did you ever rob a bank or kill someone?"

She began to realize that my line of questioning was outrageous and not meant to accuse, but to make a point. She even laughed a bit as she responded, "No."

I even asked if she had ever tripped an elderly lady trying to cross the street. She giggled and replied, "No."

Then I asked the big question—the one that would have even made me squirm in my seat: "Did you ever have sex?"

Her face became flushed and the eyes that were so big, now looked away in disbelief at hearing the very word "sex." Chuckles and surprised laughter circled the pews like a wave and slowly subsided. She looked at me and rolled her eyes again, "No. Of course not."

The point of my interrogation: Imagine innocent little Morgan, at age 12, being the only person left on the earth who never drank or did drugs, never killed anyone or robbed a bank, never tripped an old lady or had sex outside of marriage. Even she, in order to go to Heaven, would not be good enough. The only way Morgan will enter Heaven will be the same way it is now and has been for thousands of years. Jesus, who is God and became man and took nails in His hands and feet while being hung on a cross, still says, "You can't do enough on your own. You're sinful and you need to be forgiven. You are the reason I died. That's how much I love you." Even Morgan, as innocent as she was at 12 years old, needed a savior. Even she needed to set aside her pride and become a charity case. For only the Lamb of God can take away the sins of the world.

Morgan softened as she realized my lesson was not meant to embarrass her; it was an illustration to expose all of humanity's need for Christ, no matter how innocent we may appear. I looked at Morgan, "I hope you know that you should never do drugs, get drunk, rob a bank, or have sex outside of marriage."

She nodded in agreement.

"But most of all I want you to know this," I said. "In order for you to go to Heaven, you need to have Jesus in your heart. He is a free gift from God, and if you haven't received Him yet, then just say, 'Jesus, I want You. I know I can't earn Heaven on my own and I need to be forgiven.' I want that for you, Morgan."

And I want that for everyone, including you. You can't do enough on your own. The gift has to be received.

ENDNOTES

1. "Americans Donate Billions to Charity, But Giving to Churches Has Declined," Barna
(2004) www.barna.org;http://www.barna.org/. Giving USA 2004, AAFRC Trust for Philanthropy (2003). *Giving & Volunteering in the United States 2001,* Independent Sector (2001).

2. Jim Henson, Sesame Street, *Ernie & Bert Can, Can you?* (Westminster, MD: Random House Children's Books, 1982).

3. Michael W. Smith, "Give It Away," lyrics found at: http://www.sing365.com/music/lyric.nsf/Give-It-Away-lyrics-Michael-W-Smith/FF3A0E6BC68A9C374825692E000A00B2.

4. J.I. Packer, *Rediscovering Holiness* (Ann Arbor, MI: Servant Press, 1992), 149-150.

CHAPTER 3 DISCUSSION QUESTIONS

1. What do you think the statement, "If you aren't a charity case, you're not a Christian" means?

2. Would you rather give help or receive it? Why?

3. Do you think some people have taken advantage of charity? Can that happen with God's grace?

4. What are the perks of receiving the gift of grace and saying that you need God's love?

5. Do you think people can live out their Christianity on their own? Why or why not?

6. What did Jesus do for us that we could not do for ourselves?

MORALITY BASED CHRISTIANITY

I am shocked that you are turning away so soon from God, who called you to Himself through the loving mercy of Christ. You are following a different way that pretends to be the Good News but is not the Good News at all. You are being fooled by those who deliberately twist the truth concerning Christ. Let God's curse fall on anyone, including us or even an angel from heaven, who preaches a different kind of Good News than the one we preached to you. I say again what we have said before: If anyone preaches any other Good News than the one you welcomed, let that person be cursed. Obviously, I'm not trying to win the approval of people, but of God. If pleasing people were my goal, I would not be Christ's servant (Galatians 1:6-10 NLT).

> *I do not treat the grace of God as meaningless. For if keeping the law could make us right with God, then there was no need for Christ to die* (Galatians 2:21 NLT).

I have this against myself—I've been called to return to my first love. I felt God saying to me, "Bob, go back to loving Me. That's what it is. It's got to be Me, Jesus, not morality." The focus of our life cannot be morality, because for many, the focus becomes a Christian lifestyle instead of Christianity. It's got to be Christ. There is an appearance-based Christianity that looks very Christian, that doesn't flow from a relationship with Christ. That's not Christianity; that's a lifestyle.

I'm often asked how I got started speaking in public schools and other events around the country. Many people think it was a dream of mine since childhood, but that is far from the truth. Don't get me wrong. I can't imagine doing anything different with my life now than bringing a message of hope to youth. It's more than a job or obligation to me; it's my passion, and I feel called to do it. But in reality, the calling that now burns in my bones had a very humble and unassuming beginning. It all came about quite by chance.

My brother, Bill, a pastor, was asked to speak at a convention of high school students in Stevens Point, Wisconsin. He had spoken there previously, and they asked him to return. Bill called the church group contact person to apologize that he couldn't make it and suggested that I, his little brother, present the program instead. It seems a little odd to me now, thinking back. The person probably thought, *Hmmm. Your brother, huh? Well, we've never heard of him, don't know if he's any good, and we're not sure what he's going to say.* But, OK. So I went and spoke to a workshop of about 20-30 young people. I joke with my brother now and tease him about how he was never asked back, but I was the keynote speaker the following year.

Anyway, after I first spoke in Stevens Point, a girl approached me. She was a freshman, a little freshman. She wore a football jersey as though it were a nightgown. It came down to her ankles and draped over her shoulders. The sleeves were rolled up to reveal hands that gestured as she spoke. She was very enthusiastic and talked as though she had just consumed a six pack of Mountain Dew.

"I'm going to get you to speak at my school," she said.

I was surprised at her forwardness, but replied with skeptical enthusiasm, "That's great! Good!"

She could tell I hadn't exactly taken her comment seriously. "You don't believe me, do you?"

I felt a little uncomfortable when she called my bluff. My wife, Carol, was standing next to me and looked at me with a grin that said, "Well, dear? Aren't you going to answer?"

I gained my composure and replied, "Well, it's just that I've never done that before."

She had a look of determination in her eyes, and challenged me with my own words. "I thought if you had faith all things are possible," she said.

I had used those very words in my speech that day. *I hate it when they listen,* I thought sarcastically. "Well," I said, "if you can set it up, I'll come."

I left that day honestly expecting to hear nothing more about it. But two weeks later I got a call from a counselor at Marion High School, a school in a small Wisconsin community, home to a little freshman. The voice on the other end of the phone asked, "Is this Bob Lenz?"

I said, "Yeah."

She said, "Do you speak to high school students?"

I grew nervous, realizing the little freshman took my words to heart. Part of me felt a bit of delight, knowing my words had an impact. But mostly I was startled. "Well, I… I have," I said. I thought to myself, *It wasn't a lie. I just had a captive audience of students two weeks earlier! So what if that was only because my brother couldn't make it!*

"Do you do school assembly programs?" asked the counselor.

Still nervous, I replied, "I…I…I could."

She told me that any time a student wanted their friends to hear someone who would have a positive impact, the administration did its best to bring the presenter to the school.

So I began planning my talk; I was determined not to be boring, and would share what I felt God laid on my heart. My first school assembly talk was well received. They listened! When I was finished speaking, they gave me a standing ovation. Because it was a public school, I couldn't share the Gospel outright; but I shared truth. Seeing how hungry they were for truth, sharing it with them, and telling them how valuable and worthwhile they are made my spirit soar. *Huh. Maybe I should do this more often.*

I'm not a natural-born speaker. I got a C- in my high school speech class. In fact, my teacher told me never to go into public speaking. It's true. It doesn't come naturally. Although my words are not eloquent, I have a passion for youth. Young people are struggling with hurts, pains, struggles, depression, and suicide, and I want to make a difference. I want to love them, and I thought that day after my first school assembly program, If I could, I would. So I continued speaking, and the opportunities to speak grew along with my desire to reach youth with a message of hope and truth.

When my brother, Bill, was asked when his little brother became a national speaker, he said, "When he put it in his brochure." That wasn't far from the truth, but I figured since I had spoken outside Wisconsin, it was considered national. Fortunately since then, I have spoken in all 50 states. I have even spoken in my hometown school, which was really fun because when I was a student there, I was always told to shut up. Now they were paying me to talk!

SPEAKING THE TRUTH

I had the opportunity to travel with a church to Mexico on a mission trip. We were in a community helping to build a church, working with electrical wiring, painting, and general construction work. The church had services at night with about 200 people attending. It was really something to see a small community of believers on fire for God. Oh, how they worshiped! They sang with such abandon. Many of them were poor village people, but they were rich in spirit.

The Mexican preacher was very animated as he preached. It was great. When I met him afterward he said, "I heard you are a speaker and a preacher."

"A little bit," I replied.

"Would you like to speak at our sister church?"

My mind started racing over what this would mean. You guessed it—an international speaker! In my mind I could already see it in the new brochure.

I was excited to accept his invitation—not just because of the brochure, but because I had the Good News to share. Also, I had just written a new message after attending a dynamic communications workshop. Now I knew how to craft and weave words together so that people would remember. The message was called, "The Design of the Heart; the Dependence of the Heart." I felt good about how it flowed and the thought-provoking content. The pastor encouraged me to dress more formally, so I bought a tie. For this, I would want to make a good impression. After all, it was my international speaking debut!

As we drove to the sister church in a nearby village, I expected to see a similar church to the one we were in previously with 200 people in the congregation. But as we drove closer to the village I could see that the poverty we'd witnessed earlier was nothing in comparison. The other village had small shacks where families lived, and there were some with running water, a high standard of living for that area.

In this village, however, there were no such luxuries. No shacks, no water. Some "homes" were made only of a wall of bricks and a piece of sheet metal as a roof. Some people lived in cardboard boxes or beneath propped up pieces of plywood. Even the roads, if you could call them that, were barely passable and had worse potholes than an abandoned Wisconsin back road after years of heaving frosts and neglect. I began to wonder if the roads were torn up because of construction—but, no, there was no sign of any improvements being made to this destitute community. It got worse the farther we traveled.

We arrived at the church that afternoon, and I was supposed to speak at the four o'clock service. I thought they chose that time because it was a more seeker-sensitive time of the day. In reality, it was because they had no electricity to light the church for an evening service. Small, wobbly benches, that I wouldn't have used for around a bonfire, lined the church—a one-room wooden structure no larger than my bedroom back home.

I came expecting a big church like the one we had been in the night before. Rather than the crowd of 200, the rickety benches were filled with about 15 children, all under the age of 7, and two grandmothers. They were so poor. I stood stunned for a moment. There I was ready to impress a captive congregation—now I was humbled by my own arrogance. The reason they came was not because they heard there was going to be an "international" speaker from the United States, but because they knew that when they came they would be given a little bag with a wash rag, a bar of soap, toothpaste, and a toothbrush. That's why they came.

There I stood in my tie with a message that had all the strategically crafted points, Scripture references, and stories. And there they were, 15 children sitting in front of me who were more interested in getting free toiletries than hearing my speech. *I've spoken to high schools with thousands of youth in the audience, I thought. What am I going to do with these fifteen kids?*

It was then when the Spirit of God spoke to my heart. It wasn't a thundering voice like, "HELLO, BOB!" It was more like a soft, still prodding in my heart saying, "Bob, love them. Just love them." I threw my notes down and knelt beside them and hugged them. Their eyes glimmered so brightly against their dirty little faces, and their ragged clothes shook with excitement as someone showed them the type of love that wasn't afraid to dirty a brand-new tie. I had a camera with a telephoto lens, and the children were amazed by it. So we played with them. We gave them little crafted bracelets that they treasured like jewels, and told them about Jesus' love, and how we loved them too. We simply enjoyed their company, and had a great time sharing the simple love of Christ with them.

As I returned to the larger village that night, I prayed. In my heart all I could hear was, "Bob, you came to impress somebody. You came here to do a good job of speaking, and all I want you to do is love. They don't need to be impressed! Are you more concerned with impressing them or impacting them? Are you going to perform or truly love? When you're in front of a high school with a thousand students, I don't want you to be there to impress them either. I don't want your goal to be how much you can make them laugh and to see if you can make them like you. I want you to love them. They're hurting, and they need hope. They need someone to tell

> All I want you to do is love. They don't need to be impressed.

them they're loved, accepted, and forgiven, no matter where they've been, no matter what they've done, no matter what kind of family they come from."

COMMITMENT

So, that's where it all started. I wasn't a ready-made speaker. I just had a passion. I just wanted to tell people that Jesus loved them. Right then, I decided to promote life, real life, just like John 17:3 says, "This is eternal life, that they know You, the only true God, and Jesus Christ, whom You have sent."

I was convicted after hearing from God. How did I drift and end up being more concerned about "my message" than His message? How did it change from Life Promotions to self-promotion? Perhaps you know what I'm talking about? You set a goal, your focus is clear, and you know what you want, but somehow you end up in a different place with a different motivation.

Take marriage, for example. For those of you who are married, do you remember when you first met your spouse? Remember when you fell in love? Remember all those feelings? You couldn't wait to see them again and when you did, you wanted to look into your beloved's eyes. You never ran out of things to say to each other, and when you were with them the hours went by like minutes. When you were apart, the minutes seemed like days. Remember that?

I had a couple come up to me once after hearing me talk about the love between a husband and wife. "Bob," the husband said, "you know that 'love' you're talking about? We used to be in love."

I looked at both of them curiously. They seemed like a nice couple. "Well, what happened?" I asked.

They looked at each other and smirked. Then they turned back to me and replied, "We got married."

I nervously chuckled, but quickly realized their pain was real behind the half-hearted humor. "What do you mean?" I said.

They became more serious as they began sharing their story, which wasn't all that uncommon. "Well," he said, "we got married because we were in love. After we got married we moved in together, and both of us worked to buy a home, which seemed to consume our every waking moment. Then we had three children who woke up in the middle of the night and stole our sleeping moments. It seemed we never had a chance to talk like we used to."

He continued, "Then there were bills—bills for

doctors, house payments, clothes, and diapers. There were bills for things we never expected, like a new water heater and repairs for a flooded basement. So to keep up, we started working overtime and spending even more time apart. When we got home we realized the house still needed to be cleaned and vacuumed, the grass cut, the groceries bought, and the meals cooked. We thought as the children got older it would get better. But before long we had to run this child here and that child there. One of them had soccer practice and the other had a piano recital.

"Then we helped them with their homework and went to their parent-teacher conferences. Not to mention, we felt the need to be involved in church, so we helped out in Sunday school and hosted a Bible study in our home, which meant we had to clean and vacuum even more, and… Bob," he said as he came up for air, "I don't know if we know each other anymore. Sometimes I look at the person lying next to me in bed and I feel like I'm looking at a stranger. We're still married, but what happened? What happened to the love? Where is the excitement? Where is the passion?"

Now, please understand. I'm not saying that marriage is supposed to always be lovey-dovey and pure emotional bliss. But as easy as it was for me to lose my focus on loving teens, and as easy as it is to lose the romance in marriage, that's how easy it is to desert the Gospel.

A guy came up to me many years ago and said, "You're a newer Christian, aren't you." At the time I wondered how he knew. "I can tell," he said. "You have that new believer's zeal. But don't worry, it'll wear off. It's just like marriage. It starts with the honeymoon, but it's all down hill after that."

It doesn't have to be that way! If I can honestly say I love my wife more today that I did on our honeymoon, why can't that be true of my relationship with the God of the universe?

It's not just about commitment. It's about days when you don't want to get up and go to work. It's about being there and doing those tasks every day. But there's more. We start out in one place—a honeymoon, when everything looks good and we're focused and passionate. But so quickly the honeymoon is over.

I talk to men and women who long to be in love with their spouse. They long to say, "Take me on a date. Spend some time with me. Get to know me again." So how does this relate to our Christian life? I believe that the Groom of Heaven is talking to His Bride, the Church on earth. I wonder if He's not asking us some of the same questions.

*You have perseverance and have endured for
My name's sake, and have not grown weary*
(Revelation 2:3 NASB).

This is Jesus speaking—I can tell because it's printed in red in my Bible. He is saying, "Good job! Way to go! You're being faithful in your commitment! You know that faith is more than just a feeling. You're there! That's good!" It's similar to how He may be talking to you about your marriage, or the marriage of the young couple mentioned earlier. "You've been faithful. You've been making meals, changing diapers, mowing the yard. Good job! Way to go!"

But the Scripture passage doesn't end there. Jesus says, "But I have this against you, that you have left your first love. Therefore remember from where you have fallen, and repent" (Rev. 2:4-5 NASB). Remember when you were in love. Remember that! It doesn't have to be over. Commit to reviving your passion for Christ, for your marriage, for your original motivation of your goals.

PERSONAL RELATIONSHIP

I remember when I first fell in love with Jesus. I was on a retreat, and I met Jesus. I met Him as much as I can say I met one of my friends. It's a relationship. There's no way we can say we don't know each other.

We have memories together. I met Him, not just the religion. I met Jesus and I knew I was forgiven. I knew I was loved. He spoke to me through His Spirit, His Word, His people, and then through communion. It was beautiful. I met Christ. And then, once I met Him, I made a commitment to grow as a Christian.

So what does that mean? For most, the conversation in one's mind goes something like this, *Let's see, I've got to grow now. Christians…hmmm, what do Christians do? What don't they do? Well, Christians don't get drunk. OK. I'll stop getting drunk. What else? Smoking, chewing, and hanging around people who do—yes, I'll quit that too. Better business ethics at work, honesty on my tax returns, and no more cheating or lying? Done. Those sound like good Christian things to do. Wait a minute, what about the music I listen to and those magazines hidden under my mattress? Yes, I'll throw them all away and start listening to good Christian music, and reading books about God so I can find out about a bunch more stuff I should and shouldn't be doing.*

All of this is great, but it is also dangerous when our goal is no longer loving Christ, but just living like a Christian. Gradually, trying to live right replaces our relationship with Jesus. Paul warned the Galatians in Galatians 2:21—3:3:

I do not set aside the grace of God, for if righteousness could be gained through the law [trying to be good], Christ died for nothing! You foolish Galatians! Who has bewitched you? Before your very eyes Jesus Christ was clearly portrayed as crucified. I would like to learn just one thing from you: Did you receive the Spirit [become a Christian] by the works of the law, or by believing what you heard? Are you so foolish? After beginning with the Spirit, are you now trying to finish by your own human effort? (Galatians 2:21–3:3)

Have we started with a relationship with Jesus, the King of the universe, and ended up allowing our focus, the centrality of our Christianity, to drift? Has the central focus of our Christianity been Christ, the man, God in the flesh? Or has our central focus become morality? I wonder if living right has replaced our passion, our relationship, and our intimacy with Jesus.

This sums up my point: If morality is the chief goal of the church, then the Gospel is void of its power. If morality is the goal, then it's not Jesus; it's just being right. How does this happen? How do we lose focus on what matters? Sincerely ask yourself, and your heart, this question: Is it a relationship with a living God, or has it gone back to rules, religion, and routine?

As Ravi Zacharias has said, "Jesus Christ did not die to make bad people good—He died to make *dead people live*."

> *As for you, you were dead in your transgressions and sins* (Ephesians 2:1).

We were dead in our sins. We were dead, separated, and alienated from God. But Christ in His grace and mercy gave us life when He was raised from the dead. He quickened us. He made us alive! Remember how it felt when you first met the love of your life? You felt alive! Now *that's* a relationship.

Our relationship with Christ starts out sincerely, but so quickly, we go back to rules, regulations, religion, do's and don'ts. Those things need to be a by-product of our relationship, not the focus of our heart. Is it the person of Jesus, or has it become programs, performance, Bible studies, and regular church attendance?

Is it faith in a living God, the Creator of the universe, or is it facts and references to be memorized to impress others? Is it love, or is it laws and legalism? Is it dependence on God, or has it just become a duty?

Many people who have a Christian lifestyle are not living at all. They're bound in legalism and religion instead of true life. Remember John 17:3, "This is life, yes even eternal life, that they might know You, the one true God, and Your son, Jesus, whom You have sent." That's what it is, and that's what we need.

I want you to be aware of the lie of morality-based Christianity, and understand Jesus-focused Christianity. Can you define the focus, intent, purpose, and drive of your heart? Is Christ at the center of your world? Do you talk to Him daily? Does He talk to you about what you're supposed to do, who you're supposed to look like, and where you're supposed to have your focus? It's got to be Christ. Meeting Jesus changes a person. You can't stay the same.

Morality-based Christianity has three dangers— pride, a worldly attitude, self-righteousness.

PRIDE

My wife's brother and sister-in-law, John and Beth, live in Green Bay, Wisconsin. Their neighbors have a cute 2-year-old son who was given a tricycle. Now, this is not your ordinary tricycle. It had a pole attached to the back that allowed the parents to push the child on the bike. You've probably gone for a walk with your kids, and even though they're on their bike, they can't pedal as fast as adults can walk.

With this bike, the boy rode in front, believing that he

was leading the way and Mom and Dad were following him. In reality, they were pushing and directing him. The boy's eyes were filled with excitement and thrill of achievement as if he was proudly thinking, *Look what I'm doing! I'm doing a good job! But he wasn't doing it at all.*

Many Christians today have a similar attitude, "Look at me! Look what I'm doing. I'm growing in Christ." If there is any righteousness in us, it's because of Christ alone. There are two words that don't go together: pride and Christian. How can you be a proud Christian? That's an oxymoron. The opposite is true. Becoming a Christian requires humility; humility to say, "God, I'm a sinner. I don't deserve Heaven. I don't deserve to be loved by You on the basis of my good works, my earnings, my intelligence, or my knowledge. You, in Your rich mercy, have forgiven me, a wretched sinner. God, thank You."

> His prayer was focused on the trinity of me, myself, and I.

Remember the Pharisee and publican from the Bible? The Pharisee was up front for all to see, saying something like, "Thank You, God, that I'm not like other men. I pay my tithe and You know I pray three times a day." But the publican in the back shadows had his head lowered in remorse and said, "God, forgive me, a sinner." (See Luke 18:9-13.)

There are many modern-day Pharisees. They may sound something like, "Father God, I thank You that I'm not like others. Thank You that I'm not like the liberals. Thank You that I'm a part of the Christian Coalition. Thank You that I endorse prayer in public schools and oppose abortion. Father, thank You that I voted for the guy who wanted the Ten Commandments displayed in the public school-room. Lord, thank You that I listen to six hours of Christian radio every day and never miss a *Focus on the Family* program. And thank You that I signed up to automatically receive that daily devotion to my email. Thank You for Bible studies, seminars, and books. Yes, thank You, God, that I am not like others."

> Jesus is not a stance on homosexuality. He is not a stance on abortion or the church growth movement. Jesus is not a stance on worship style or evangelism.

Christianity is not defined by your political agenda. It doesn't go hand in hand. Have we reduced Jesus to a stance on an issue? Jesus is not a stance on homosexuality. He is not a stance on abortion or the church growth movement. Jesus is not even just worship, or a stance on the style of worship. Jesus is not even legalism about evangelism that may lead others to Him.

Jesus is a person to be loved, and our churches have reduced Him to a program to be followed.

Do you know Him? Do you love Him? I'm not accusing anyone stuck in the rut of legalism of not being a Christian. After all, that young couple, despite finding themselves as strangers to each other, was still married and committed; they had just lost their focus. How about your relationship with Jesus? Has your focus become unclear? Are you still in love with Him? Do you love Him more today than yesterday? Do you really know Him?

We can't be proud as Christians. Romans 9:16 reminds us that it doesn't depend on man or woman, but God. How many of us say, "Look at me riding my bike! Aren't I doing a good job!" I believe God is saying, "Hello! I'm behind you pushing. I'm the one responsible for your achievements, not you. Let Me live through you and change the world through you. Just love Me and let Me love you and see My Kingdom come."

A WORLDLY ATTITUDE

The second danger has to do with what the world tastes. What is the world's perception? I'm with non-Christians almost every single day of the school year. I've heard many times what they think of most evangelical Christians—they are bigots, proud, arrogant people with their noses up in the air, looking down on everyone else. According to nonbelievers, they think John 3:16 could read, "For God so loved the world, that He picketed it." I'm not saying we shouldn't picket against important issues as Christians. If God leads you, then be obedient. But don't allow that issue to become your Christian identity, because that's what the world will see, and that's what the world will believe being a Christian is all about. I'm so glad that Jesus didn't see us as sinners and say, "Whew. That's too sinful for me. I don't want to die for someone like that." He loved us. Why? He wanted a relationship with us.

When musician Marilyn Manson was in the spotlight, he was scheduled to perform a concert in a Midwestern city. In case you're not familiar with him and his music, he makes Ozzy Osbourne look like a saint. Christians in the city were rightfully concerned about the band's influence on the youth and the community. They started a petition to stop the concert, and gathered an amazing 22,000 signatures. Despite the effort, the concert went on. The once-struggling ticket sales skyrocketed, and the show sold out. Christians made a stand *against* immorality and sin, but did they take a stand *for* Jesus? Was His name lifted up?

Consider this approach to the Marilyn Manson concert, as suggested by a Nazarene music pastor. He wondered what Jesus would have done in this case. He pictured Jesus eating supper with the band like He did with the "unholy" people of His day. This pastor decided he could be most like Jesus by calling the arena and offering to provide an elaborate meal for the band. He thought they should be shown grace—unmerited favor. Although this approach may have been more difficult to pursue, it would have been centered on Christ's character and His mission, evidenced in the time Jesus spent with sinners while He was on the earth.

The danger is this approach: The world doesn't taste Jesus; they taste pride, condemnation, judgment, criticism, arrogance, hypocrisy, and an air of superiority. Many times, we as Christians look at someone's circumstance or sin and think, *Tisk. Tisk. That's not very Christian-like, now is it? You'd better straighten up and act like a good Christian.* It may be seen in a glance, a snide remark, or while standing on the sidewalk holding a picket sign. Our actions communicate that "they" need to clean up their act to become good Christians, as if only their definition defines Christianity. And if they don't, we won't like them, and we'll scream even louder. Worse yet, we communicate a message that tells non-Christians that Jesus won't like them either. But Jesus loves all people! Remember, while we were yet sinners, Christ loved us so much that He died for us.

Oftentimes we are killing our witness and becoming the very enemy of those whom we say we want to become our brothers and sisters in Christ. Does this mean we shouldn't speak truth into others' lives? Of course not. We need to speak the truth in love. (See Galatians 4:16.)

I simply argue that the cross should be raised at the center of the marketplace as well as on the steeple of the Church. I am recovering the claim that Jesus was not crucified in a cathedral between two candles, but on a cross between

> We're not becoming their enemies because we are telling them the truth, but because of *how* we are telling them the truth.

two thieves; on the town's gar-bage heap; at a crossroads so cosmopolitan they had to write His title in Hebrew, Latin, and Greek...at the kind of place where cynics talk smut and thieves curse, and soldiers gamble. Because that is where He died, and that is what He died for, and that is what He died about...that is where churchmen ought to be and what churchmen ought to be about. —Rev. George MacLeod of Scotland[1]

SELF-RIGHTEOUSNESS

The third danger has to do with our own experiences, and our own souls. By focusing on morality, we miss out on the most awesome relationship in the world.

When a well-known Christian television character fell, his sin was exposed in all the newspaper headlines. Everyone was talking about how it happened, and why. I heard one analyst describe why he thought the popular televangelist fell. "This guy was doing a work for God. He kept bringing all his works and saying, 'Here, God. Look!'" The analyst related the situation to a simple occurrence in his own life. He told the story of how his 4-year-old son had made him a little house of toothpicks. It was slanted to one side, lathered with glue and glitter, and set clumsily on a cardboard square. The boy presented it to his dad, "Look, Dad. I did this for you!" Dad looked at the little house, "That's really nice, son. Great job!" He took the little house and placed it on the side table next to him, reached out his arms and said, "Come on. Why don't you sit on my lap?" But the son replied, "No, Dad. I've got to go make you some more of these houses." So he went out to make another stick house.

The analyst's point: All the ministries on earth and all the things we do become opportunities to come and sit on God's lap. "Come and get to know Me," God's saying. "Fall in love with Me." But we're busy, busy, busy. I've got to fight this cause and make my point. I've got to be heard and stand up for what I believe. I've got to learn more, serve more, build more, share more, and become more. More what? It's time to sit on His lap. It's time to fall in love with Jesus and say, "You're the only One who matters."

Let's repent of pride. Let's stop thinking we need the world's approval; let's stop judging others according to our personal definition of Christianity; and instead, let's do what Jesus did, "For God did not send His Son into the world to condemn the world, but to save the world through Him" (John 3:17).

Let's focus on our relationship with Jesus and allow Him to be our heart's desire. That's what is going to make the difference in this world.

ENDNOTE

1. Ron Ferguson, *George MacLeod — Founder of the Iona Community* (Glasgow: Wild Goose Publications, 2001).

CHAPTER 4 DISCUSSION QUESTIONS

1. Read Galatians 1:6-10 and Galatians 2:21. What do you think Paul was warning the people against?

2. What is the difference between trying to impress somebody or love somebody?

3. Think about the story about the boy who thought he was riding the tricycle on his own when his dad was actually pushing him. What are ways we have done this in our own Christian life? How do we take credit for what God is doing?

4. This chapter says it's an oxymoron to be a "proud Christian." Do you agree? *Can* you be a proud Christian? Why or why not?

5. Explain what morality based Christianity is.

   - What are the three dangers of morality based Christianity?

6. How do we promote a moral lifestyle without allowing it to become more important than Jesus?

UNCONDITIONAL LOVE 5

The unconditional love of God: It's more than a theology to be studied, more than a doctrine to be understood. It's a subject that can't fully be comprehended. It's better than any romance movie. It's what our hearts long for, that there is a person at the center of this truth, of this theology. A belief that He is also the creator of the universe and that He is, in reality, pursuing me. That makes my mind spin. Here is a collage of my thoughts and hopes, a collection of my internal conversations and spiritual interactions, hoping to allow my spirit and soul to encounter God's love, moving beyond just theory, to experiencing it firsthand. I hope the same for you as you read it. I pray you come face to face with Him and His unconditional love.

Unconditional Love...

Too good to be true.
But it is. Only in fairy tales.
Not so.
What's the catch?
None.
Beyond my wildest dreams.
But it's in real life.
For others, but not me.
Called you by name.
Can't be.
Is.
Won't last.
Yes, forever.
What are the odds?
Sure thing.
What must I do?
Nothing.

A love without conditions.
No strings attached.
Known, understood, wanted, chosen, pursued, the apple of His eye!
His cherished possession.
His treasure.
Accepted for who I am.
Forgiven for what I've done.
Not wanted for what I have.

Not picked for my accomplishments.
Welcomed just as I am.
Not chosen because of my talents.
Embraced in my undeservedness.
Not His by my own doing.
Secure by His promise.

These words are mine because of
unconditional love:
Free
Forgiveness
Gift
Justified
Grace
Salvation
Mercy
Ransomed
Favor
Cherished
Redemption
Loving Kindness
Faithful
Compassion
Unmerited
Undeserved
Generous
Thoughtfulness
Understanding
Helpful

Passionate
Sensitive

Unconditional love…
My goodness didn't earn it!
My sinfulness cannot lose it!

Unconditional love…
My works did not grant me access to it.
My failure can't keep me from it.

Unconditional love…
My knowledge did not obtain it.
My foolishness couldn't misplace it.

Unconditional love…
My desire didn't possess it.
My carelessness can't undo it.

Unconditional love…
My righteousness didn't merit it.
My selfishness didn't cancel it.

Unconditional love…
My prayer didn't deserve it.
My lust didn't nullify it.

Unconditional love…
My integrity didn't secure it.

My wandering didn't invalidate it.

Unconditional love…
My serving didn't attain it.
My murderous thoughts couldn't stop it.

Unconditional love…
My Bible reading didn't acquire it.
My doubt didn't withdraw it.

Unconditional love…
My religion didn't reach it.
My idolatry didn't restrain it.

Unconditional love…
My tithing didn't buy it.
My jealousy didn't negate it.

Unconditional love…
My obedience could not obtain it.
My anger did not repress it.

Unconditional love…
My kindness did not win it.
My drunkenness did not destroy it.

Unconditional love…
My self-control did not reach it.
My fornication and adultery did not cancel

it.

Unconditional love…
My church attendance wasn't payment for
it.
My absence didn't dispose of it.

Unconditional love…
My commitments didn't warrant it.
My divorce didn't annul it.

Unconditional love…
My contentment didn't coax it.
My anxieties didn't scare it away.

Unconditional love…
My meditation couldn't realize it.
My strife didn't interrupt it.

Unconditional love…
My vows didn't justify it.
My shame could not hide it.

Unconditional love…
My best cannot deserve it.
My worst has not, and will not
destroy His love for me.

I am unconditionally loved…period.

Case closed!
Verdict given!
It is finished!
Over.
Done deal.
Irreversible.
No appeals!
Proclaimed as fact!
Loved...
Accepted...
Forgiven...
Forever!

Unconditionally loved?
Yes.
Face it!
Deal with it!
Reject it if you will, but that doesn't
change the fact...
You are loved.
By faith, receive it.
Believe it.
Count on it.
By faith, cling to it.
Repeat it.
Proclaim it.
Trust it.
Enjoy it.
By faith, sing of it.

Dance because of it.
Shout it!
Let that truth of love free you!
Fill you!
Forgive you!
Let it empower you,
Enrich you,
Encourage you!
Let it help you,
Hold you,
Give you hope!

Unconditional love…

There is nothing quite like unconditional love. Once I tasted it, nothing could ever satisfy me again…as if it ever really satisfied me before. At times I thought I felt satisfied, well at least in part. But it never lasted; it was only a partial, temporary fulfillment. You know? Like…

From the respect of recognition…to the accolades of accomplishment.

From the commendation of conquest…to the pride of possessions.

All fades in importance when I'm searching for what matters most.

All the things of earth grow strangely dim in the light of His glory and grace…

Unconditional love.

It comes down to relationships. Relationships are what matter, what count.

From fun fellowship, to the depth of friendship.

From the heart of a parent, to the bond of siblings.

From daily companionship, to the intimacy of lovers in marriage.

Relationships, for all they were meant to be and mean to us, even at their best are only a shadow, a fraction, an imperfect, tainted replica of what it was meant to be with Him. At their best…our hearts really long for, were designed for, and will only be fulfilled with… unconditional love.

But then, I need to be realistic and return to earth where I live. To me, even an imperfect, tainted replica of real love is more than I ever allow myself to dream of, or fantasize about, much less hope or long for.

Leave that to the young and foolish, the writers of fiction. Or, to be perfectly honest, leave it to the few, the brave, the chosen, the Jones', or…the delusional.

For what was meant to be in relationships in my life is not only imperfect, but it's broken into pieces beyond recognition to the natural eye. Dreams shattered into slivers so small no one by any condition would deem worthy, or of value, or of any dignity. Who would want what I have?

Yet I can't face this reality. I can't handle this.

The lack of purpose. The lack of meaning!

There must be more—more to this life.

Is this what it's all about?

The search intensifies. I must find something, some One.

The hunger grows and my pace is accelerated out of a need to belong.

My thirst is exaggerated to where my wants are mixed up with my need, and my life becomes busier and busier in pursuit of the American Dream of life, liberty, and the pursuit of happiness.

I've never had so much, yet felt so depleted.

Never have I been so surrounded by so many people and felt so alone.

Never have I had so much to do, yet felt so little sense of contentment.

The vain pursuit of accomplishment and possessions make me cry out as a leech, crying for more…

SIN equals
Still In Need.
Never satisfied.

More!

> The wages of sin is…more!
> Because it's never enough.
> **SIN** equals **S**till **I**n **N**eed
> Never satisfied.
> Void.
> Emptiness.
> Lack.
> Vacuum.
> Nothingness…

These are the words that now describe my soul, my being.

I'm reduced to just a human doing. My wants now own me.

I'm an apprentice to the Trumps of society, only to leave us both bankrupt once again with my cry for "luck to be a lady tonight" going unanswered yet again.

Yet I hear society cheering me on...

"Don't give up!"
"Believe in yourself."
"You can do it!"
"Stay positive."
"Determination."
"If at first you don't succeed, try, try again."

So I muster up all I have left that resembles hope...
a little more guarded, protected, cautious.
I call it wisdom from the school of hard knocks.
If I were honest...
I'd call it desperate.
Now I live in a fantasy of the future saying,
This time it will work...
This person is different.
This church.
This job.
This marriage.
This pregnancy.
This town.

This friendship.
In search of peace, hope, love.

I dull my senses with comforts, thrills, and romantic stimulation.

Thus the market for more…

Romance novels
Time shares
Bigger homes
Vacation/cruises
Promotions
Cars
Theme Parks
Internet
Video Games
iPhones
Learn in your sleep
Add an inch
Lose weight
Renew your sex life

Yet with the law of diminishing return, few find the feeling of home, the unconditional love their hearts are looking for. Why would I be any different?

The result?

The soul no longer feels its worth.

Hopelessness has taken up residence.

Struggle and survival are now the only signs of life.

Some would insist that this isn't life at all.

It's just existence.

Now instead of living life to the fullest, I just endure another day.

Learning how to settle for less, I betray my original design and desire. I sell out. I give in. I succumb to the weariness within and the pressure without.

Denial is my only comfort. Escape is my only solitude. Harmony is left to the orchestra, and not for my inner being. I have become one with my universe and the confusion now spins me round and round the sun, but I feel no warmer.

All I can now call a feeling is anger.

I feel cheated, deceived, ripped off!

Contempt changes direction toward others…human-kind, organized religion, politics, my parents, my wife, and then…myself.

I'm not good enough.

I deserve this.

Finally, my anger is directed at God…

How could a God of love let this happen?

Is it chance?

Maybe there is no God.

But even the whining grows old and I become numb.

I'm growing hard, dying from the inside.

Depression, a sense of darkness, now looms over the emptiness.

Helplessness screams for release but finds nothing inside of me that can make things better.

It only insists there's no way out.

Worthlessness now personified takes on a personality of its own, mocking me for ever thinking things could have been different for me—me, of all people.

It flashes my mistakes over and over in my mind, stripping me of any last feeling of a remnant of value.

"Why even care," whispers a newcomer.

Worthlessness introduces her friend...

Apathy.

"I'll take it from here," she says in a vague and eerie voice. "There's no need for you to do a thing. It wouldn't matter anyway. You're finished. Everything they said to you was true. They were right, so don't forget what they said." So, with a belittling voice filled with insults and put downs, the old sayings come back and never seem to end, going over and over in my head…

You knew better.

What were you thinking?

You idiot!

I told you that you would never amount to anything.

Way to screw it up again.

Did you really think someone would want you?

Loser.

You're pathetic.

You disgust me.

I told you you'd never be as good as your brother.

I didn't expect any more of you.

You are such a disappointment.

You're a waste of space.

I don't even know who you are!

I told you…I told you!

You'll never learn.

Don't even talk to me.

How could you?

Look what you've done.

I hope you're happy now.

Silence. (Neglect)

It's your own fault.

What did you expect?

You're no ordinary dummy.

Don't touch me.

Get away from me!

Shut up. I don't even want to hear it.

Excuses, excuses, excuses.

Now I've heard it all.

What next?

Did you think nobody would find out?

How stupid can you be?

That's what you get.

I hope it hurts.

You made your bed, now sleep in it.

You're only getting what you've got coming.

You fool.

You're good for nothing.

You're a piece of work.

Who would ever love you?

What am I going to do with you?

You're giving me a headache.

You are a pain in the ass.

You're like a pebble in my shoe.

I'm not even going to waste my time with you.

To me, you don't even exist.

I warned you.

I told you she was no good.

It figures. Why do I even get my hopes up?

You're nothing but a piece of trash.

You stink.

Your own mom doesn't want you.

It would have been better if you were never born.

I wish I would never have met you.

Can't you do anything right?

You're an accident waiting to happen.

Did I ask for your opinion?

You're getting on my nerves.

It's your own fault.

You're only getting what you had coming.

You were an accident.

You're not my kid.

Go play in traffic.

Shame on you.

I hate you.

I didn't know they piled crap so high.

You're just a failure.

Pack your bags.

You're out of here!

Don't ever come back.

I never want to see you again.

I feel sorry for your family.

You're an embarrassment to everyone you know.

Don't you have a decent bone in your whole body?

Go tell someone who cares.

You're morally bankrupt.

You're sick!

You're just plain evil.

You're a poor excuse for a person.

Ha, ha, ha, ha…

Look at you…

Na, na, na, na…

I want a divorce.

It's over!

There's someone else.

I don't love you anymore.

You're not worth it.

You're boring.

You're ugly.

You're not good enough.

We picked someone else.

You're fired.

We're downsizing.

We don't need your services anymore.

Beat it.

You blew it.

I don't care.

Voices, voices, and more voices affirm my feelings of worthlessness.

Ever been there? I have. Maybe you're there right now. You're not alone. Countless people have been there.

Unconditional love...Change is impossible on our own. Righteousness is impossible on our own. Merit is impossible on our own. Holiness is impossible on our own. Salvation is impossible on our own.

With people it is impossible, but not with God; for all things are possible with God (Mark 10:27 NASB).

Because of...

Jesus.

More than a teacher,

More than an example,

More than a man…

He is Emmanuel.

God with us.

The Savior of the world.

The world!

That includes you and me.

Evidence of grace in a believer's life is…

Gratitude.

God did for me what I didn't deserve and what I couldn't and still can't do for myself.

When I heard that Good News for myself, when I heard His word, it was saying to me personally, "You are loved beyond your wildest dreams; even in spite of your lack of hope."

When I heard it was real, my heart flickered.

When I knew my goodness didn't merit it and my sinfulness couldn't prevent it, my heart ignited!

Like a thrill of hope…a weary heart rejoices.

You, too, will fall on your knees when you hear it, really hear it.

And your heart will beat as if for the first time. New life.

Humanly, I can't even fathom that this is true.

But somehow I believe…

That's faith! Beyond me—outside myself.

More than normal—above the natural—a sense of wonder.

My spirit breathes its first breath.

A ray of light, a sign of life—real life.

A sense of, "Could it be?" It is.

Authentic, genuine…Unconditional love.

My soul cries out as a newborn…

"Yes! Yes! This is what I've been waiting and longing for!"

What I was made for.

Created for.

Designed for. Just this…

Relationship.

It's like someone breathed new life into me.

Awakened me from a deep sleep.

Rescued me from an enemy.

Raised me from my deadness.

Called me into a new story.

Beckoned me to come on a new journey.

Softened and molded my hard lump of clay.

Wrote a new ending to the play of my life.

Painted a different backdrop and called me His masterpiece.

He called me His beloved.

Chosen.

Precious.

How could this be? Yet I somehow am driven to, almost made to…

You see?

It's irresistible…

I believe.

I believe!

I know my failures, yet I stand forgiven.

I know my past, yet I have a future.

I know I don't deserve it, but it's assured.

I know my depravity, yet He's given me dignity.

I know my weakness, yet sense a strength.

I know my shortcomings, yet feel complete.

I have a reason, a purpose, and at the same time, a peace and a rest. I belong.

Yet, I am called to action.

I know it's OK to just be, to be the me I was meant to be.

My value is not in who I am, but whose I am.

And why?

Not because of what I've done, or not done, but because of who He is and what He's done.

He has made a way to enter into a relationship with Him—the God of the universe.

God is love, and He created me to share in that love. I was designed to bring glory to God by enjoying Him forever.

Starting now.

Knowing His love alone brings fulfillment, peace, worth, value, joy, lasting hope.

Knowing Him is life, for He is the one true God.

The only way to obtain that relationship is through what He did by loving me unconditionally through His Son, Jesus.

Unconditionally loved?

Yes.

CHAPTER 5 DISCUSSION QUESTIONS

1. On a scale of 1-10, with 1 being God's love is a theory and 10 being you've experienced it, where are you on the scale and why?

2. What are some things that make it hard for you to believe that God really loves you?

3. Look at the list of words on pages 111-112 about unconditional love. Do these words remind you of anyone? Who has demonstrated unconditional love the most to you in your life? How?

4. Pages 126-128 contain belittling voices from people in the past. Pick one or two negative statements that you struggle with and explain why.

5. If God really loves us beyond our wildest dreams, why do so many people not experience it?

6. Explain what this statement from page 133 means: "My value is not in who I am, but in whose I am"?

7. How do people's lives change when they know they are loved unconditionally?

GOD IS NOT A TRADITION

6

A 4-year-old girl walked into a Christian bookstore. She was ecstatically proclaiming, "I'm going to Heaven! I'm going to Heaven!" The owner of the bookstore knelt down on her knees to celebrate with the little girl. "That's great," said the smiling bookstore owner. "You're going to Heaven because Jesus loves you." The little girl's joy turned into defensive sternness. *"No!* I'm not going to Heaven because Jesus loves me. I'm going to Heaven because I said the prayer," she said with attitude in her voice. Then she continued, "My little brother's not going to Heaven because he didn't say the prayer."

This story makes me angry because it shows how we have reduced the Gospel of Jesus down to a sinner's prayer. I've even heard the sinner's prayer called "eternal fire insurance." Prayer, instead of communicating or connecting with God, has become something that needs to be done—a requirement that gets us into Heaven—and thus becomes a work that needs to be accomplished to gain favor with God.

If there is something self can do to attain salvation or justification, then salvation is not by grace alone. This is why many people call today's Christianity *decision theology,* which warns us of a human-centered gospel, which is no gospel at all. The Gospel means "Good News," and there is no good news for humankind except for cross-centered Christianity.

In some Christian circles, to determine a person's journey of faith, often the question asked is, "If you died today, would you spend eternity in Heaven?" If the answer is *"Yes,"* then the question is, "Why?" or "Because of what reason or merit?" If the answer begins with, "Because I…," I would say there is not a clear understanding of grace and salvation. The answer should begin with, "Because God…." The focus must be on what God has done, not on what we do to merit our salvation.

My brother, Tim, was severely handicapped; he never spoke a full sentence. I don't believe that when he died he went to hell because he didn't say "the prayer." That theology doesn't coincide with

Scripture or the character of God. That is one reason I love the theology of infant baptism that says, "God has claimed you as His own, unconditionally, undeserving, you are called, chosen, made part of the family, not on your own doing, but by another. Your parents, standing in your stead with the church (Christ's presence on earth), have marked you by the water and Word and set you apart based on Christ's death and resurrection.

I know people who believe in adult baptism by immersion, following the order they see in Scripture to believe and be baptized. They see it as an outward sign of an inward work of God; a sign of commitment, as a wedding ring is to marriage. They make a commitment to follow Christ, to make a public proclamation of their beliefs, indicating they're taking their faith seriously. This is what I love about adult baptism, for it is personal and they are not ashamed of the Gospel of Jesus. They profess this belief in the context of their faith community.

Yet my concern is, I know a person who was baptized four times because "This time I'm serious about God." My frustration is that the focus is on the person and not what God has done. When my brother, Tim, was born after a three-day intense labor, he had a high fever and wasn't expected to live through the night. The priest rushed to the hospital to baptize him, for if Tim was not baptized before he died, he would go to hell. This belief limits God to being merely an act of water sprinkled on a baby's head. Sacrament? Yes. Magic? No.

In Dr. C.F.W. Walther's book, *The Proper Distinction Between Law and Gospel,* he states it this way:

> The gospel merely says "believe and thou shalt be saved," while the law issues the order: "Do this and thou shalt live." Now, if the mere act of being baptized and partaking of Holy Communion brings grace to a person, the gospel manifestly has been turned into a law, because salvation then rests on a person's works. Moreover, the law has been turned into a gospel, because salvation is promised a person as a reward for his works.*1*

I am angered and frustrated thinking about how this holy sacrament of baptism has become false life insurance for many parents who believe their kids are safe because of it, instead of trusting in a loving, faithful, wise, and just God.

Unfortunately, being baptized, communed, and confirmed, and completing all the required church stuff, doesn't guarantee that the youth have experienced or established a personal relationship with Christ. In many instances there is no evidence of genuine faith. Many times they just go through the motions expected as the cultural norm of the group instead of enjoying faith-filled actions from the heart.

You can honor the traditions of your denomination and still nullify the Word of God by producing only lip service.

> ...*Thus you nullify the word of God for the sake of your tradition* (Matthew 15:6).

> *These people honor Me with their lips, but their hearts are far from Me* (Matthew 15:8).

I've heard it said that evangelism must start within our own churches. For within our pews on Sunday morning, our Sunday schools and youth groups, there are a number of baptized non-believers. The Bible says believe and be baptized and you will be saved. Believe not and you will be condemned. (See Mark 16:16.)

CONTROL

I'm not here to defend one tradition or to tear down another. The core issue is control. We want a formula—steps to obtain God's grace. We want to explain, teach, and understand how God works, to put God into our box as if He were a thing to be contained. God is a person to be loved, not an object to be theorized, or an equation to be figured out. The Gospel is simple, but when we oversimplify it in areas of application, we insult the educated, expose our ignorance, and blaspheme the God who is all-knowing. The Gospel is so simple that a child can understand it. Still, it's such an amazing mystery that the smartest people in the world can't explain it.

> **God is a person to be loved, not an object to be theorized, or an equation to be figured out. The Gospel is simple, but when we oversimplify it in areas of application, we insult the educated, expose our ignorance, and blaspheme the God who is all-knowing.**

...their hearts will go out to you because of the surpassing grace God has given you. Thanks be to God for His indescribable gift (2 Corinthians 9:14-15).

You see, with real grace—God's indescribable gift—the issue is not having it all figured out. It's a matter of faith, a matter of trust. We must foster theology and tradition in a way that leads to a faith relationship with Jesus. In the spirit of Christian love, we respect the practices of different people and different denominations. God's grace is extended to all, not just a chosen few.

> That God was reconciling the world to Himself in Christ, not counting men's sins against them. And He committed to us a message of reconciliation. We are therefore Christ's ambassadors as though God were making His appeal to us. We implore you on Christ's behalf, be reconciled to God (2 Corinthians 5:19-20).

Are we bringing people and Jesus back together, or are we so hung up on our way of explaining it and our own pet doctrine, that we never get to what matters?

When I was in the 7th grade I went to an interdenominational outreach event. I had a powerful spiritual encounter and was moved by God's Spirit through the music, testimony, and sharing of God's Word. I responded to the call, and afterward I was directed to pray with an adult. I sat down with the adult; we were facing each other. He asked, "Is this your first time or a recommitment?"

"A recommitment."

"When were you born again?"

"I'm not sure of the date," I said.

A look of disgusted panic came over his face and he said, "What's your natural birth date? When were you born?"

"May 13, 1963."

He said, "See, you know when you were born the first time. If you really knew the Lord, you'd know when your spiritual birthday was. You're not a Christian yet. You're not a saint; you're still a sinner."

I sat stunned and embarrassed. This is a true story. And I have heard so many, too many others just like it.

ONLY GOD

When the Power of One, an event cosponsored by more than 15 denominations (not just individual churches), was being coordinated, the Catholics and Lutherans said, "If you're having an altar call, we're not going to be a part of it." The Baptists said, "If you're not going to have an altar call, we're not going to come." Some Four Square and Assembly of God people wanted to know if they could have a special time to pray for the young people to have a Pentecostal experience.

I love theology and love to discuss and debate; yes, even argue. But I have to wonder if we have not hurt the cause of the Gospel with our special-interest mentality. Please don't get me wrong or misquote me. I think we need to study the Word of God and be grounded in our faith, and know what and why we believe, to be a Berean of the Word. But can't we center our lives and church's beliefs on the person of Jesus and the Gospel; the life, death, and resurrection of Jesus, the author and finisher of our faith? Can't we agree on the essential doctrines the church has upheld for over 2,000 years identified in the Apostles' Creed?

I'm thrilled that for the past 24 years, the Power of One has proven that a variety of churches can agree on the Gospel's essentials. Several thousand youth from dozens of different denominations attended each year. *Woe to any of us who set up hoops to jump through and terminologies to be understood and become fluent in, expectations to meet and manmade rules to follow, a theology that reduces God to a formula and practices, and alienates rather than welcomes outsiders. There is only one way unto salvation—Jesus.*

> *Jesus answered, "I am the way and the truth and the life. No one comes to the Father except through Me"* (John 14:6).

No matter what tradition or denomination we come from, may we not exclude people because they don't understand our practices. Through understanding where they are spiritually, let's invite them into a relationship, or a deeper relationship, with Jesus. Many feel far away from God, not experiencing His forgiveness, but feeling alienated and condemned, because of misunderstandings or terminology. Instead of seeing the grace that is available for all, they see it as something available to only the few who can grasp the complicated descriptions and definitions we have given it.

After giving a talk on forgiveness at a camp, a 16-year-old guy came up to me. His shoulders were caved in, and his feet shuffled along the floor with his head hanging low. He couldn't even look me in the eye as he talked to me. He told me that my message didn't apply to him.

"I can't be forgiven," he said. "I knew what I was doing was wrong and I did it anyway. There's no forgiveness for me."

"Yes, there is," I said.

But he insisted, "No."

I tried to assure him that no matter what it was, the Lord still loved him and had already forgiven him 2,000 years ago on Calvary. His blood cleansed every sin, no matter what.

"I'm a pastor's kid," he said. "I know what the Bible says. I think this is the unpardonable sin."

Again, to no avail, I told him if he had committed the unpardonable sin, then he wouldn't care. The only unforgivable sin, after all, is rejection of God's free gift in Jesus. Nothing he had done had changed God's heart toward him. It's not as though any good he had done before this "big" sin had appeased God's wrath against all his other sins. Even before this happened he hadn't met the requirements God had given to acquire Heaven outside the Gospel. Only a perfect life and keeping the whole law could do that. And that was something only Jesus had ever done.

My feeble words and thoughts on theology brought no comfort to his soul, or release of the guilt he felt. Was he undeserving? Yes. A sinner? Of course. Aren't we all? So, no big deal? Wrong! Huge deal. Sin is worthy of death, damnation, and hell. Sin is the essence of the problems on earth, the enemy of our soul. It's like putting water in the gas tank of a car, but worse;

it's fatal. It's eternal. But God, through the redeeming grace of Christ, forgives our sin.

"I started to go to parties just to fit in," he continued. "I was sick of being the Christian kid, the P.K., the one who was holier-than-thou. So I just started doing what everybody else did. It was fun. I would just hold a beer, and it felt great to fit in. Soon it became an every-week thing. Then I met this girl and she really took an interest in me. She wasn't a Christian, but we started to date anyway. My drinking increased. I was starting with at least a six-pack a night. One night after a party I drove my girlfriend to her home. She told me her parents were gone and asked me to come in. My spirit was telling me to say no. I knew it wasn't right. My whole being was screaming, 'Yes!' It's as though I mouthed 'no,' but 'yes' came out."

He continued, "It's not what you think. It wasn't just lust or sex. I really believe I loved her. It was beautiful, intimate, and unbelievable. I tried to convince myself it wasn't wrong, and I was even mad at God. I wondered why He would be against this. Yet, the next morning when the alcohol wore off, the guilt came with regret and wouldn't go away. So I thought, *I really messed up, so why even care? Why try to resist?* So we did it again. See Bob, I knew it was wrong, but I did it anyway—more than once. How can God forgive me?"

When I tried to say something comforting, he interrupted me and said, "Stop. That's not all. There's more. It gets worse, OK? She became pregnant. I didn't want anyone to find out, so I paid for an abortion. I took my girlfriend to the clinic and I paid to have my own child killed!"

I held up a Bible and asked, "Do you believe this is God's Word?"

"Yes," he said.

"Really?" I asked. "You really believe this is true?"

"Yes, that's why I believe I can't be forgiven," he said.

"Do you believe God can lie?" I asked.

"No," he said.

I opened the Bible to First John 1:9 and said, "Read this."

He read it out loud: "If we confess our sin He is faithful and just and will forgive us our sins and purify us from all unrighteousness."

When he finished reading I asked, "Does it say He might forgive some?"

"No," he replied.

I looked him in the eye and asked, "What does it say?"

"He will forgive *all*."

"Doesn't that include your sin?"

"Well, yeah, but…" he said.

I interrupted, "Yes or no? True or false? Forgiven or not? Loved or forgotten? Does it include you?"

"Yes," he said. Then the tears came—healing, cleansing, forgiving tears. Washed by Jesus' love from the inside out. Grace. Unconditional love.

What was his response? Gratitude. He didn't say, "Great, since I can be forgiven it doesn't matter how I live." No, God granted him repentance. The Greek word for repentance is *metanoia*, "a change of mind and heart." God's Word being proclaimed instilled faith. And the goodness of God led him to repentance. That's why they call it the Gospel—the Good News.

…do you think lightly of the riches of His kindness and tolerance and patience, not knowing that the kindness of God leads you to repentance? (Romans 2:4 NASB)

That's why preaching repentance of sins is part of the Good News. We can't repent on our own power. Repentance is a gift, just as much as forgiveness is. God granting us repentance is part of His unconditional love.

This young man was afflicted in his soul. He knew what he did was wrong. He needed comfort, not more condemnation. He was one who, I believe, Jesus would have called captive, one who needed to be set free. Jesus is the truth that sets us free.

RECEIVE FORGIVENESS

How about you? How do you feel when your sin is exposed? Or maybe you live in fear because you're afraid that

> Repentance is a gift, the same as forgiveness is a gift of God.

someday it may be exposed. If they really knew. The hiding. The guilt. The shame. There's an ache in your stomach when you're honest with the depth of the sin you've committed, or the level of selfishness you've displayed, or the motives behind what you do. The lust that you can't tame. The bitterness, the hatred, the anger, the insecurity. Think of the amount of energy you use every day just pretending, trying to uphold your reputation, or that of your family, your business, your church, or community.

If you have been where this young guy has been, you feel like a disgrace; you can't look at people in the eye; your head hangs down; you try to run and hide. Your face turns red; your mouth is dry. You think, *How could I? Why did I?* You feel like a dog that made a mess in the house—your tail is between your legs and there's nowhere to hide. They grab you and rub your nose in it. Perhaps it's when your husband found the half-empty bottle of vodka in your drawer; the 900 number that showed up on your credit card bill; the loss of your family's savings and house at the casino; the night you don't remember, but someone else does; your insider trading of stocks; the kid you baby-sit for told her parents what you did; you failed the drug test…again; you were spotted coming out of a hotel with another woman; your wife found out about your sexual involvement with another man; you used the "f" word when you yelled at your daughter in front of her friends; you were caught shoplifting; you were caught masturbating…at Bible camp.

Remember First John 1:9 doesn't say He might forgive some, it says He will forgive all.

AMAZING GRACE

"Amazing grace, how sweet the sound, that saved a wretch like me."[2] This old hymn has stood through the ages as a testament to God's grace. God's grace is big enough even when you feel like a wretch.

A friend of mine told me a story about a funeral service she attended. They celebrated the man's life and spoke on the grace of God. It was a beautiful time of reminiscing and rejoicing in the new life he was now experiencing, void of pain and sickness. When it came time to sing, the beautiful hymn "Amazing Grace" was played on the organ. The words were printed on the back of the program for people to sing along. "Amazing grace, how sweet the sound, that saved a one like me…" The word *wretch* was replaced with *one!* Why?

Are we afraid we're going to offend someone by pointing out their sin and calling it what it really is—wretched?

> I've heard it said that if sin isn't that bad, then grace isn't that good.

If we can't admit that we are, in fact, wretched, then His grace isn't all that amazing!

When you feel like a wretch and you don't measure up, when you've been exposed, caught, or just sick and tired of hiding, and you just can't try any harder, remember that God is a God of amazing grace.

> You saw the misery of our ancestors in Egypt, and You heard their cries from beside the Red Sea. You displayed miraculous signs and wonders against Pharaoh, his officials, and all his people, for You knew how arrogantly they were treating our ancestors. You have a glorious reputation that has never been forgotten. You divided the sea for Your people so they could walk through on dry land! And then You hurled their enemies into the depths of the sea. They sank like stones beneath the mighty waters. You led our ancestors by a pillar of cloud during the day and a pillar of fire at night so that they could find their way. You came down at Mount Sinai and spoke to them from Heaven. You gave them regulations and instructions that were just, and decrees and commands that were good. You instructed them concerning Your holy Sabbath. And You commanded them, through Moses Your servant, to obey all Your commands, decrees, and instructions. You gave them bread from Heaven when they were hungry and water from the rock when

they were thirsty. You commanded them to go and take possession of the land You had sworn to give them. But our ancestors were proud and stubborn, and they paid no attention to Your commands. They refused to obey and did not remember the miracles You had done for them. Instead, they became stubborn and appointed a leader to take them back to their slavery in Egypt! **But You are a God of forgiveness, gracious and merciful, slow to become angry, and rich in unfailing love. You did not abandon them,** *even when they made an idol shaped like a calf and said, "This is your god who brought you out of Egypt!" They committed terrible blasphemies. But in Your great mercy You did not abandon them to die in the wilderness. The pillar of cloud still led them forward by day, and the pillar of fire showed them the way through the night* (Nehemiah 9:9-19 NLT).

> You are a God of forgiveness, gracious and merciful, slow to become angry, and rich in unfailing love. You did not abandon them...

This is the Old Testament! God has always been a God of grace. His grace is sufficient for you.

Some people teach Acts 15:1 wrongly, which says, "…Unless you are circumcised, according to the customs taught by Moses, you cannot be saved." Sound familiar? "Unless you know the date when you were born again…." But Acts 15:9 says God "cleansed their hearts by faith." Paul asked, "Now therefore why do you put God to the test by placing upon the neck of the disciples a yoke which neither our fathers nor we have been able to bear?" (Acts 15:10 NASB). You can almost hear Paul screaming, "No! It's only through grace. God's Word assures it!

> **I will not shrink back from sharing lavishly and freely that grace abounds to all.**

> As far as the east is from the west, so far has He removed our transgressions from us (Psalm 103:12 NASB).

> …Though your sins are as scarlet, they will be as white as snow; though they are red like crimson, they will be like wool (Isaiah 1:18 NASB).

You are justified…God sees you as if you never

sinned. There are many who live with self-hatred, self-contempt, guilt, and shame. They are bound by the aftermath of thought, desire, and actions. For when our sin abounds, God's grace abounds much more.

> ...*where sin abounded, grace abounded much more* (Romans 5:20 NKJV).

I know my heart and I know my thoughts. I know my past. I know my secrets. And I know the only chance I have to survive is by grace. He is a loving, gracious God. If you do not believe me, look at Him. See how He has treated sinners like you and me. His name is Jesus, and He treats us with that same love today.

"Bob, it sounds like you're being light on sin," said a friend of mine. All I can do is bring it back to the Word, and to the Word who became the perfect expression of the law of God lived out—Jesus, who came, taught, breathed, and lived God's heart. For He was and is God's heart—the great I Am, forever, and ever, and ever. Many miss what God is saying today, just as many missed God's grace that was present in the Old Testament, and when they were face to face with Jesus.

> *As He was speaking, the teachers of religious law and Pharisees brought a woman who*

had been caught in the act of adultery. [Where was the man? It takes two.] They put her in front of the crowd. "Teacher," they said to Jesus, "this woman was caught in the act of adultery. The law of Moses says to stone her. What do You say?" They were trying to trap Jesus into saying something they could use against Him... (John 8:3-6 NLT).

I wonder if they thought, *Jesus, You're going to be light on sin, aren't You? What about the Torah? What about God's standard and His teaching? What about tradition?* But Jesus bent down and started writing on the ground with His finger. Why did He bend down? Could it be because the woman's eyes were staring down? Could she have felt like the dog that made a mess in the house and was waiting for the moment when they would rub her nose in it, punish her, and banish her from their sight? Was she recoiled in fear and expecting Jesus to further expose her shame? Instead, Jesus wanted her to feel the comfort of His words, and to bring the prideful eyes of the teachers down and humble them. Their eyes

> Because God has not been stingy with me, neither will I hold back or be stingy with the grace that has set, and is setting, me free from my past, present, and future sin.

were diverted for a moment, away from the woman and focused on the scribbling of Jesus.

Oh, to know what He wrote! Was it secret sins of those around Him? Were they words such as pride, arrogance, and judgment? Or did He write: justice, mercy, and faithfulness? As they continued to question Him, He straightened up and said, "If any one of you is without sin, let him be the first to throw a stone at her." Again, He stooped down and wrote on the ground.

Jesus is left alone with the woman. The older ones left first, and then the young zealous legalists. Jesus stood up and asked her, "Woman, where are they? Has no one condemned you?" She answered, "No one, sir." (See John 8:7-11.)

Only Jesus remained. He is the only one who fits the description of "Him without sin." He is the only one qualified to stay and confront the woman. Only Jesus has the right to throw the first stone. But He didn't. Jesus says to her, "Neither do I condemn you."

THE LAW

You may think she got off too easy—that she needs to know there are consequences for the choices she made. Did Jesus say adultery was OK? As far as we can tell from the story, this woman had no visible signs of repentance. She was caught. She didn't come clean on her own. The teachers of the Law and Pharisees did what the Law was supposed to do—bring people to Jesus. The Law in itself doesn't make us holy. It slays you and tells you you're guilty. It says you missed the mark, you deserve to be killed. Remember the last time someone said, "You know better than that!" Knowing right and wrong doesn't always keep you from doing wrong.

> Oh, I hope you can hear it; listen closely...the sound of each stone as it fell to the ground, with a thud of hope.

The Law as God intended is good, holy, pure, and needed. Its intent is to bring us to the end of ourselves and to the feet of Jesus—the only pure, perfect one. So, does anything go? No.

> The Law's intent is to bring us to the end of ourselves and to the feet of Jesus.

Jesus doesn't condemn the woman; He condemns her sin. He also condemns the sin in the Pharisees and teachers who thought their sin wasn't as bad as hers. She was broken and felt helpless.

When we were utterly helpless, Christ came at just the right time and died for us sinners. Now, most people would not be willing to die for an upright person, though someone might perhaps be willing to die for a person who is especially good. But God showed His great love for us by sending Christ to die for us while we were still sinners. And since we have been made right in God's sight by the blood of Christ, He will certainly save us from God's condemnation. For since our friendship with God was restored by the death of His Son while we were still His enemies, we will certainly be saved through the life of His Son (Romans 5:6-10 NLT).

> Grace doesn't say that it doesn't matter how good you live. It says that no matter how good you live, it's not enough.

Our attitude can't be: We are the good people and they are the bad people who need Jesus. We need to use God's Torah, His law, not to condemn others with the sins that sicken or disgust us, but to let the Law bring them and us into the daily presence of Jesus, for we need constant instruction and grace. Human nature would rather have a good lifestyle and average faith rather than a life of brokenness overflowing with faith. When we allow the Law to be effective in our lives, we are humbled and broken people who beg for Christ's mercy.

In Phoenix at a rehab center, I was speaking to drug addicts, alcoholics, prostitutes, and criminals who were out on parole. Life had beaten them down; they were a broken people.

> Human nature prefers a good lifestyle and average faith rather than brokenness and overflowing faith.

To my surprise, the fellowship was sweet, for all they had to cling to was Jesus. There was no judgment, just acceptance, love, and grace. I wondered why I didn't experience that type of sweet fellowship in some of the churches where I'd spoken. Instead, I often see facades, playing church, politics, and a lot of maintaining an image; faith that is moderate at best.

I wondered, *If my kids had to go through abortions, addictions, and hardships to really find an in-depth relationship with Jesus, or instead, I could choose to have them be upstanding, cultural, successful people with pride and pharisaical attitudes, which path would I pick for them?* Sadly I'd choose the upstanding lifestyle. Being honest, I'm still more committed to an image of an intimate relationship with Christ than I am to a genuine faith that results from experiencing the amazing grace of God, a grace that can only be known by someone who can admit their wretchedness.

I was telling my son, David, who was 10 at the time, that he was named after my father, but also after David in the Bible, who was a man after God's own heart.

"David, I want you to be like that; like David in the Bible."

"Dad, are you sure?"

"Yeah, follow God, whatever it takes."

"OK, but I don't think I should be like David in the Bible in everything.

"Yes," I assured him, thinking of a message I had given on David and his passion for God.

"Okay, Dad. But did you know David broke all ten of the commandments?"

"No, no. Don't be like him in *that* way!" I exclaimed.

David told me that he had been studying about King David in Sunday school that week.

I wonder how close David in the Bible would have been to the Father's heart without first struggling with the wretchedness of his own heart. That's not what God intended. I know He doesn't want or expect us to break all the Commandments. God's plans are plans to prosper us for good, not to harm us. (See Jeremiah 29:11.) God does not enjoy seeing His greatest creation hurt by the hard realities of this life and the consequences of our bad choices.

When our circumstances and our choices bring pain, shame, or guilt, I believe the Father weeps with us, and that He feels our infirmities. He sees our darkness. He sees our wandering. He sees when we're abused. He sees our hearts bleeding. His *Ten*-der *Commandments* show us how to live. But no matter how hard we try, it's just not enough. So we're rendered without excuses and we have to admit the bondage of our sin. Not even Houdini could escape the chains and the darkness of death. God is so big; God is so loving that He redeemed and bought us back. He'll make good, even out of bad.

> *As for you, you meant evil against me, but God meant it for good...* (Genesis 50:20 NASB).

God is so big that nothing can separate us from His love, not even our sinfulness, not even our darkness.

Yes, His Law has warned us, given us loving teachings, the Torah, for our own good. Even before the Law of Moses He gave us laws that would keep us from harm. For example, Adam and Eve could eat of any of the trees except the one. He always gives clear instructions to live by.

Again, grace doesn't mean, "No more rules or guidelines." Grace never means, "Throw out the Law," as if to imply that the Law is bad, and grace is a license to sin. Grace doesn't free us to sin. Grace frees us *from* sin. The problem is in us, not in the Law. The Torah hasn't failed. We have. Humankind has gone astray. Every person on earth is accountable to the law—God's universal standard. Some argue that God doesn't have situational ethics. But His definition is different than the world's definition. He has unchanging ethics that apply to every situation based on the unchanging truth of His word. He never changes. Many people believe the Old Testament is Law and that the New Testament is grace. Not true. The Old and New Testaments are full of law and grace, as shown earlier in this chapter in Nehemiah chapter 9, and in the following Scripture passages.

> **Grace doesn't free us to sin— grace frees us *from* sin.**

...I will show mercy to anyone I choose, and I will show compassion to anyone I choose (Exodus 33:19 NLT).

...But let me fall into the hands of the Lord, for His mercy is very great. Do not let me fall into human hands (1 Chronicles 21:13 NLT).

In panic I cried out, "I am cut off from the Lord!" But You heard my cry for mercy and answered my call for help (Psalm 31:22 NLT).

Come and show me Your mercy, as You do for all who love Your name (Psalm 119:132 NLT).

Let the wicked change their ways and banish the very thought of doing wrong. Let them turn to the Lord that He may have mercy on them. Yes, turn to our God, for He will forgive generously (Isaiah 55:7 NLT).

Where is another God like You, who pardons the guilt of the remnant, overlooking the sins of His special people? You will not stay angry with Your people forever, because You delight in showing unfailing love (Micah 7:18 NLT).

Jesus says, "You must love the Lord your God with all your heart, all your soul, all your mind, and all your strength" (Mark 12:30 NLT). When I ask people if that verse is Law or Gospel, people almost always respond, "Gospel, Jesus said it." Look again. I believe it is Law. Remember that Jesus was responding to a question about the greatest Commandment! Loving God is something we are commanded to do by our Lord and Savior, Jesus Christ.

The New Testament is full of law, full of Torah. Law and Gospel don't oppose each other; they complete each other, yet they are separate. Every sermon must contain both. And every Christian must learn how to divide law from Gospel, and how to clearly distinguish between the two. The Law says do; the Gospel and grace say done.

I've heard it said that John Calvin stated, "The law *could* make us righteous if any of us *could* keep it." This is where my anger burns against my own arrogant pride and that of the church legalists. We have used the Law to point out certain sins of society and cleaned up the outside of our own lives enough to feel good about ourselves, and created an "us and them" mentality. Thus there is a good versus bad; saint versus sinner; holy versus defiled; pure versus unclean; saved versus lost; righteous versus unrighteous mind-set within the church as a whole. We've forgotten to cling to the fact that the condition of all society is the same as the state of our condition outside of Christ.

The Law doesn't condemn only the pedophiles, the divorced, those who have had an abortion. The Law condemns us all, renders us all without excuse, and excludes us all from the promise of life. I am both a sinner *and* saint, good *and* bad at the same time. With this being true, I can't take a posture of pride toward others. The Law brings us all to the same level.

> The Law says do; the Gospel and grace say done.

When G.K. Chesterton (1874-1936) was asked what the problem with the world is, he answered, "I am."[3] As much as we'd like to convince ourselves and others otherwise, there is sin that remains in us and not just in "them." That's true for all humankind. Period. The only solid Rock I can build my hope on is Jesus' blood and righteousness. I am still amazed by that kind of grace—it truly is indescribable.

ENDNOTES

1. Dr. C.F.W. Walther, *The Proper Distinction Between Law and Gospel* (St. Louis: Concordia Publishing House, 1989).

2. John Newton, "Amazing Grace," 1779.

3. G.K. Chesterton, *Orthodoxy* (Colorado Springs, CO: Waterbrook Press, 1994, 2001).

CHAPTER 6 DISCUSSION QUESTIONS

1. Why did the story of the little girl who said she is not going to heaven because Jesus loved her but because she said "the prayer" make Bob so angry?

2. Explain the difference between a works theology and a grace theology.

3. Explain the purpose of the law.

4. Has anyone ever kept the whole law?

5. Have you ever felt unforgiveable? What changed your mind?

6. Did Jesus come to die for just the good people?

7. Read Romans 5:6-10 and describe the human condition when Jesus died for us.

8. What is the Gospel, or Good News, in your own words? How would you explain it to someone who has no clue about God or the Bible?

   - How is it possible that the Gospel can be so simple that a child can understand it, yet so complex that the wisest people can't fully articulate it?

THE DARK SIDE OF GRACE

I will give you the treasures of darkness and riches hidden in secret places... (Isaiah 45:3 NRSV).

Most of us are not willing to embrace the darkness inside ourselves. We like to blame outside factors: today's music, the government, a political party, terrorism, Islamic extremism, racism, or poverty. Jesus told us that it's not what enters a man that defiles him, for out of the heart come evil thoughts. (See Matthew 15:17-19.) To admit that sin is a condition of our hearts and that we're helpless to change it on our own is the key. It is in this place where the treasure our heart longs for will be found.

C.S. Lewis asked, "Why must the holy places be dark places?"[1] Like Lewis, I don't understand why either;

yet Psalm 18:11 says, "He made darkness His covering, His canopy around Him." How God chooses to share His grace with humankind often takes my breath away and leaves me pondering the love that was willing to enter the darkness for me.

> To admit that sin is a condition of our hearts, and that we are helpless to change it on our own, is the key to salvation and peace within.

At noon, darkness fell across the whole land until three o'clock. Then, at three o'clock Jesus called out with a loud voice, "Eloi, Eloi, lema sabachthani?" which means, "My God, My God, why have You abandoned Me?" And the curtain in the sanctuary of the temple was torn in two, from top to bottom. When the Roman officer who stood facing Him saw how He had died, he exclaimed, "This man truly was the Son of God!" (Mark 15:33-34,38-39 NLT).

The darkest moment of history was when He who knew no sin became sin for us; when Jesus embraced suffering, shame, sin, death, and hell, when Love died, when Life breathed its last breath. The entrance to grace has always been and will always be through the darkness of brokenness and humility. Only then will the veil be torn, releasing the light of God, the experiential presence of His Spirit, the peace that surpasses understanding, and the joy that is unspeakable. We cannot take away the darkness by ourselves, for the God who is light alone reigns over darkness. Yet at the same time

> **The entrance to grace has always been and will always be through the darkness of brokenness and humility.**

He is in the darkness with you. Trust Him alone in the darkness and with the darkness inside of you.

TUNNEL OF DARKNESS

I was coming off an airplane as I had done a thousand times before. The passengers were instructed by the flight attendant to watch our step because there was snow on the jet way. Looking down to make sure I wouldn't slip and fall, I didn't notice that the ground crew had not lifted up the door completely. At six foot four inches, I hit my head and jammed my neck—the impact threw me backward. The pain was immediate, sharp, and shot down my arm. I tried to shake it off, but the pain worsened.

This seemingly insignificant accident threw me into

a tunnel of darkness I didn't even know existed. The doctors diagnosed a herniated disc in my neck, pinching a nerve that caused the most excruciating physical pain I had ever experienced in my life. I searched for relief from several doctors. I tried chiropractors, massage therapy, traction, exercise, prayer, counseling, pain relievers…all with no relief. I took pain medication like candy, to no avail. I was given surgical shots in the hospital with medicine that was directly injected near my spinal cord. Nothing helped. I even had to cancel speaking engagements, something I've only done a handful of times in my 20-plus years of speaking, but never consecutively. I had to instruct my office to cease booking engagements.

I always knew that I didn't measure up to God's Law. But at least I was trying. The dark side of grace took away even my feeble attempts to try and measure up. The dark side of grace says that nothing we do can earn, deserve, or merit God's love or forgiveness. There is no such thing as deserved grace, merited mercy, or earned favor in God's sight. It is not in what we do. Our value is not in our accomplishments, but in what has been done for us on the cross.

I know this is starting to sound redundant, but repeating something very important is never a bad thing. I knew that God's grace is sufficient—I knew this in my head, but when the pain grew so intense, I couldn't find this truth in my being. For nearly two months I was unable to do anything. I thought I was going crazy. When it dragged on and on, I became depressed. I felt helpless. Nothing I could do, and nothing the doctors did, brought relief. It came to the point when I felt hopeless and worthless.

> Our value is not in our accomplishments, but in what has been done for us on the cross—through grace.

I had worked in suicide prevention for 20 years. When I described my thoughts, I realized that I was describing a suicidal person. I actually started to think that I would rather be dead than endure more pain. When I realized that my total focus was on me, I felt guilty, on top of all the pain, for being so selfish. It consumed me until all I could think about was me, my pain, my situation. Then I became crabby. I was so angry that it was hard for others to be around me. I couldn't be a good dad. I couldn't throw a football or play disc golf, or even listen to the songs my kids would play on the piano. I wasn't able to even sit long enough to watch a movie. I couldn't be a good husband. The pain completely wrecked a vacation I had planned for my wife's birthday in Hawaii. I couldn't be a good friend or fulfill my role as a speaker or the leader of Life Promotions. I was failing in all areas of my life.

Doubts and questions intruded on my faith, and I even felt as if I was a bad Christian. The shame was building, and I felt far away from God. When circumstances beyond my control took me out of my normal routine, I realized at the core of my being that I was still relying on my actions for my worth and value. My standing as a person, as a Christian, was dependent on me rather than on who God is to me.

When I was down and out physically and emotionally, I felt like God was far away. Realizing this exposed the sick thinking and belief in the depth of my being—when I was a "good Christian" God would love me more, He cared more, and was more personal. If I was handicapped physically or socially, I believed deep down that I would lose His favor, His concern, and forgiveness. Somehow, His love for me became based on "If I live right and do the right things," and not on His crucifixion.

This was one of the darkest times of my life, brought on by pain and physical limitation. Looking back, I had been there before prompted by other losses: death of loved ones, sin in my life, blocked goals, and disappointment.

I am sure that there have been, or will be, dark times in your life. I hate the dark. I'm afraid of the dark. I want so badly to avoid it at all cost. Yet the darkness in my soul is scarier, and even darker, than the dead of night. Maybe that's why so few admit that this is the condition of their hearts apart from Christ.

> *The heart is deceitful above all things and beyond cure... (Jeremiah 17:9).*

No wonder it is so rare to obtain the treasures found only by embracing the darkness within.

FACING THE DARKNESS

Have you ever been at a retreat, conference, or camp, or in a service when the preacher is being used by God? His words reflect the Word. His stories are used to inject the Holy Spirit's conviction. The Spirit exposes the depth of your heart and its motives. It strips away the excuses, disarms your attempts to blame others, yet will not allow you to settle for self-contempt. God's Law is lifted high and the gavel of judgment comes down. The verdict is given and you confess.

Now the pure Gospel should be preached and the gift of repentance and forgiveness offered. The preacher should extend grace to the downtrodden, beat-up sinner. Instead of this, he turns it up a notch. "Will you give it all; not 70 percent, not 80 or even 90? Will you make a 100 percent commitment to God?"

Self eagerly and enthusiastically says, "Yes, *I* will. *I* will be more committed. *I* will do it. *I* will give more. *I* will try harder. *I* will read more. *I* will pray more. *I* will sacrifice more. *I* will be a promise keeper. *I* will live for God." People leave the conference thinking, *I will give it all I've got.* And this time it works…

Guilty.

For about a week. Ever been there? Now what? One of two things will happen—you either try to "make it" on your own power, or you beat yourself up with self-contempt.

When your enthusiasm wanes, you attend another conference, festival, or movement, and *self* tries again and again. *Self* goes from one event to another seminar, to another book, to another formula, just to keep *self* going. *Self* keeps trying to make it, get it, arrive, attain, and reach that point of being 100 percent. The focus is on self, not the King, not the Kingdom, and not the lost.

Some actually convince themselves that they made it. There are denominations believing they don't sin anymore after coming to a full, true relationship with Jesus. Others think that in order to be sold out for Jesus, to have given it all to Him, means you can only affirm the new man. Any attempt to look at the sin that remains would be criticized as negative. It looks obvious here, but this attitude is subtle. Arrogance sneaks in and assures us: *Even if I'm not at 100 percent, at least I'm not like so and so.*

The arrogant become loud about that which they oppose (usually something they're secretly struggling with), and the feeling of being right fuels them. They feed their ego by making comparisons. They become more and more addicted to performing in socially accepted areas; whatever their society wants them to be. They're seen boasting with a plastic veneer of humility about how long they spend in prayer and reading God's Word, and how often and where they attend an "on fire" church. They have internal and sometimes external badges from their hours of volunteering and service. This so-called zeal for God is the life support of their denial.

I have seen this attitude in myself. I have found that my desire to be holy is the very thing that blinds me to the sin that remains. Martin Luther said, "He was blinded by a perverse zeal for God." He thought that the pride of our commitments, perfect righteousness and high service to God, were equal to the denial of our sin.[2]

Because I spend most of my time sharing the Gospel

with the non-churched, Christians often ask me after an evangelistic rally, "How many commitments to Christ did you have tonight? How many recommitments?"

WRONG QUESTION

I believe commitment to the Lord is a good thing. I hope we all grow in our commitment to Him. And I wish I could devise a way that could truly assure everyone that they are 100 percent committed to God once and for all.

But let me ask you the right question: When you die and stand before the God of the universe, do you want to stand before Him on your commitment to Him or on His commitment to you? I hope the answer is as clear to you as it seems to me. It is *His* commitment that saves us, not our own. Grace can be received or rejected. Receiving a gift is a passive response that comes from a giver who offers the gift to someone with empty hands, an attitude of humility, and a heart of gratitude.

We don't have to deny the sin that remains. We don't have to pretend there is no darkness. With our own commitment, enough is never enough. If we're bound to legalism, then Galatians 5:3 tells us we then need to be obligated to obey the whole Law. There has been, and ever will be, only one perfect One. His name is Jesus. Stop the show. It's OK to admit where and who you really are—even if you're not where you wish you were, or others think you are.

SELF-CONTEMPT

On the other hand, when facing the darkness, many give in to feelings of "I'm not good enough." Instead of putting on the front of arrogance and hypocrisy, the works theology convinces them to give up. "You're never gonna make it anyway," is whispered in your ear. You think, *Maybe God hasn't chosen me. Maybe I'm not part of the elect. I don't hear His voice. I must not be His.* These people end up walking away from the church, faith, and Christ—even though Jesus has never walked away from them. They don't feel like they belong, and don't feel accepted because they don't fit the cookie-cutter Christian image.

> My desire to be holy is the very thing that blinds me to the sin that remains.

I've heard them say things like, "I'll never be as good as so and so." I want to scream, "So and so isn't as good as they want you to believe!" These people who live in self-contempt don't hear the truth, so they give themselves to their jobs, appearance, working out, adventure, possessions, and relationships—rather than facing the dark side of grace. They look to anything and everything to keep themselves busy so they don't have to face the darkness of disappointing themselves and God yet another time. Many others just give in, saying, "If you can't beat 'em, join 'em," and they dive into the overt pleasures of the world we live in.

DARKNESS OF SELF

Both of these responses are attempts to avoid dealing with the darkness of the real self; whether that be the legalist, moralist, Pharisee, or the self-contemptuous person who has given up. We all need grace. There is enough grace for the legalist and overt sinner alike.

There is a passage of Scripture that has continued to perplex me over the years.

> *This is the message we have heard from Him and declare to you: God is light; in Him there is no darkness at all. If we claim to have fellowship with Him yet walk in the darkness, we lie and do not live out the truth. But if we walk in the light, as He is in the light, we have fellowship with one another, and the blood of Jesus, His Son, purifies us from all sin. If we*

*claim to be without sin, we deceive ourselves
and the truth is not in us.* (1 John 1:5-8).

This passage in First John tells us that God is light and that in Him is no darkness at all. Yet verse 6 says that if we claim fellowship (say we're Christians), yet walk in darkness, we lie and do not live in the truth. Verse 7 goes on to say that if we walk in the light as He is in the light, then we will have real fellowship and the blood of Jesus His Son purifies us from sin.

Wait a minute! Read it again. It's so confusing! It says we can't walk in the darkness or our faith is a lie. But *if* we walk in the light we'll be purified of sin. But I thought that if you were in the light you wouldn't sin. So then why do we need to be purified? Sound like a paradox? Exactly. It is. Verse 8 tells us that if we claim to be without sin, the truth is not in us. The reality: I can want so badly to be right and be in the light that I act like all the darkness is gone. I either pretend it's all OK and wear my Christian mask in an attempt to hide the remaining darkness, or I try to hide in the darkness itself by giving in to hopelessness.

AVOIDING THE DARKNESS

The beginning place in the journey of walking in the light is admitting where we are and confessing the dark that remains. The journey of purity and genuine holiness is paved with the acknowledgements of the "undoneness" of our souls. It means my sin is a very real part that will free me. Neither trying harder nor giving up deals with the darkness. Both are still focused on self and a works theology.

> **The journey of purity and genuine holiness is paved with the acknowledgments of the undoneness of our souls.**

Let's take another look at the story of my two months of excruciating pain. When I was down and flat on my back, I was self-centered and needed to experience grace that was bigger than my actions. I still need that—a grace that is bigger than my sin, and oh, so much bigger than my own good deeds, my own works, and my own self-deceiving arrogance that thought God loved me because I deserved His love.

Those who believe this falsehood will struggle with pride and judgment of others, believing that others don't deserve to be forgiven, or we judge them by saying, "How can they be a Christian if they..." or "They knew better than that!"

I need to believe in a love that is bigger than my choices, and even bigger than my obedience. I want to one day obey because I am unconditionally accepted for who I am (a sinner), and what I am (a sinner), and for once believe I am His child (a saint), forgiven, loved, and wanted because of what He has done. I want to freely receive His grace and then obey because He first loved me.

How in the world can people call this compromise? Again, I will say it: It's not that I am condoning sin. I am just saying that no matter how hard I try, I can never earn His love. I am saying that while lying flat on my back in anger, doubt, selfishness, and failing as a person, as a human and as a Christian, I was no less loved than when I gave a speech in His name and saw many come to faith. He is all in all. I want to stay in the position of helplessness, even now when I am back on my feet doing well. I want glory only in His workmanship, a by-product of grace. It is truly amazing. When your life is shaken, you are brought to the core of what matters most.

A dear friend of mine, Tim Soerens, once said, "Only in admitting the truth of what is, do we release the truth of what can be. Accepting what we are not is the door to becoming who we can be." The entrance to grace is still, and will always be, through the darkness of brokenness and humility.

ENDNOTES

1. C.S. Lewis, *Till We Have Faces: A Myth Retold* (Harcourt, Brace & Company, 1980).

2. Martin Luther & Johann Friedrich, *A Commentary on St. Paul's Epistle to the Galatians* (Harvard University, English & Co Smith, 1860).

CHAPTER 7 DISCUSSION QUESTIONS

1. Read Matthew 15:17-19. Explain according to this passage where evil comes from and why you believe this is true.

2. Do you believe everybody has darkness in their heart or are they just the victim of their circumstances and society. Why?

3. What does Bob mean when it says we need to face the darkness?

4. The entrance to grace has always been through darkness, brokenness, and humility. Can you explain why this happens?

5. On a scale of 1-10, if 1 is you get your identify from what you are doing and 10 is you get your identity because God loves you, where would you be on the scale? Why?

6. How do we get our identity from God and not the things we do and yet still do our best?

7. "My desire to be holy is the very thing that blinds me to the sin that remains" is this true and how does our desire to be holy blind us?

8. Bob says commitment is a good thing. Does our commitment to Jesus save us?

9. Have you ever struggled to believe that God could forgive you and struggled with self-contempt? Maybe you feel like you aren't good enough for God to love?

10. Can you be a sinner and a saint at the same time?

BACKSLIDING TO GOOD WORKS

8

Ever since I've been a Christian I've had a desire to serve God. I've always wanted to please God and be all that He wanted me to be. Backsliding was not an option. Images in my mind of backsliders include: Lot's wife turning into a pillar of salt as she looked back at the world, or the verse in Second Peter that the preacher would speak of with a fire of warning in his eyes about being sucked back into their old lifestyle, and how they were just "like a dog returning to its vomit" (2 Pet. 2:22). These images have been used to warn us to never allow sin to own us again, to try harder, and to stay pure.

As I have studied the Scriptures, though, I have seen backsliding in a different light. I see it now as a picture of a prisoner of war who hears a declaration that the war is over, and has his chains removed. Now, he is free to worship God, free to serve, free to love, free to live; to live a life of freedom through grace led by the Spirit. The requirements of the Law were fulfilled. The war is over. He's been called to walk by faith. It's a new journey—a journey many times of mystery; a journey of dependence upon God. But as he starts the new journey, fear breeds words of doubt and uncertainty, asking the question once posed by C.S. Lewis in the book *The Chronicles of Narnia—The Lion, the Witch, and the Wardrobe*: "Is He safe?" The Spirit prods in response, "No. But He's good."[1]

Some still prefer the safety of bondage to the Law (the wrong use of the law). They prefer that to an unpredictable wild ride of grace with a God they cannot tame into their box of theology. They are afraid to recklessly abandon the old, and yet abandoning it is where life is found. All too soon, they put the chains back on. It's similar to the people of Israel wandering in the wilderness who said, "At least we had food in Egypt." Or, "I want go back to the old way."

As I study Scripture I see a people, the Jewish people, who were given a promise 430 years before receiving the Law from Moses. That's what Galatians 3:8 is talking about.

The Scripture foresaw that God would justify the Gentiles by faith, and announced the gospel in advance to Abraham: "All nations will be blessed through you" (Galatians 3:8).

The people of Israel were given a covenant. God, in His grace, gave it to Abraham; but some Jewish people in the Old Testament mixed up the intent of the Law. They thought the inheritance was dependent upon their ability to keep the Law. It wasn't. Even from the beginning, receiving God's promise was not dependent upon the Law, for then it would not be based on His promise, but instead on our ability to keep the Law. Galatians 3:11 says, "Clearly no one is justified before God by the law." God kept His promise and fulfilled the law at the same time, all through and in the person of Jesus.

PROMISE BEFORE THE LAW

Take a look at some Scriptures pointing to who Jesus is: Jesus, Yeshua Hamashea, the Messiah, the Hope of Israel, the Promised One:

> *Do not think that I have come to **abolish** the Law or the Prophets; I have not come to **abolish** them but to **fulfill** them (Matthew 5:17).*

> *…God has brought to Israel the Savior Jesus, as He **promised** (Acts 13:23).*

> *You are the Messiah, the Son of the living God (Matthew 16:16).*

Christ redeemed us from the curse of the law by becoming a curse for us, for it is written: "Cursed is everyone who is hung on a pole" (Galatians 3:13).

You are priest forever in the order of Melchizedek (Hebrews 7:17).

(for the law made nothing perfect) and a better hope is introduced… (Hebrews 7:19).

Christ is the end of the law so that there may be righteousness for everyone who believes (Romans 10:4 NRSV).

The Scripture foresaw that God would justify the Gentiles by faith, and announced the gospel in advance to Abraham… (Galatians 3:8).

In response to the Gospel being preached and according to God's promise, Jews and Gentiles were coming to faith in Jesus, receiving eternal life, becoming believers, and being guaranteed a place in Heaven.

I have shared a message with youth for several years about grace and the fulfillment of the Law. We even created a shirt at Life Promotions to serve as a message reminder. It shows three ways you cannot become a Christian or earn Heaven.

#1 GE

No, it doesn't stand for General Electric. It means **G**ood **E**nough, based on the New Living Translation of Galatians 2:16. We become right with God, not by doing what the law commands, but by faith in Jesus Christ…for no one will ever be saved by obeying the law.

I once heard a pastor delivering a children's sermon, and he asked the kids, "How do you spell God?" All the children answered correctly, "G-O-D." The pastor had a felt board where he placed the letters carefully. He went on to ask, "How do you spell *Good?*" The children responded confidently, "G-O-O-D." The pastor said, "Yes!" He slid an "O" in between the letters on the board and exclaimed, "See, if you put another "O" in God, you'll be good, and then you'll get to be with God." This story causes me to fume with anger and disappointment every time I think of it. It only emphasizes the unintentional agenda of many leaders and parents as well. Sometimes we can have such a desire for our children to be good and stay out of trouble that we compromise sharing the truth of Scripture that tells each one of us that being in right standing with God is not dependent on how *good* we are. Being good enough will never be enough. No, not one is good—all have gone astray (see Rom. 3:12).

#2 RR

While it's fun to say RR with a lot of vigor like Johnny Depp in the movie, *Pirates of the Caribbean*, this RR doesn't have anything to do with pirates. It refers to the **R**eligious **R**oad. I think it was the musician Keith Green who first coined the phrase, "Just because you're in a garage doesn't make you a car." I would add that just because you're at McDonalds, doesn't make you a hamburger...but you will smell like a French fry.

The point: Just because you go to church and say your prayers, doesn't make you a Christian. The people Jesus had the most problem with were the people who had a religious arrogance. Jesus opposed those who thought they were better than everyone else because they looked so good on the outside and performed all the rituals and followed all the traditions. They were snobs who looked down on anyone else who didn't quite measure up and show the same dedication and vigilance as they did. They hid behind church doors, while publicly displaying their involvement in planning committees, Scripture memorization, tithing, prayer, and a host of other compulsory routines. Jesus refers to people like this in the Bible when He speaks of a group of Pharisees. They were relying on taking the religious road to God, and the result is once again seen in this passage in Luke.

> *To some who were confident of their own righteousness and looked down on everybody else, Jesus told this parable: "Two men went up to the temple to pray, one a Pharisee and the other a tax collector. The Pharisee stood by himself and prayed: 'God, I thank You that I am not like other people—robbers, evildoers, adulterers—or even like this tax collector. I fast twice a week and give a tenth of all I get.' But the tax collector stood at a distance. He would not even look up to Heaven, but beat his breast and said, 'God, have mercy on me, a sinner.' I tell you that this man, rather than the other, went home justified before God. For all those who exalt themselves will be humbled, and those who humble themselves will be exalted* (Luke 18:9-14).

There are a lot of people on the religious road who will be quite disappointed when they come to the end of it, only to find that it was a dead end.

#3 KIA

KIA is not referring to the car with a 100,000-mile warranty. That's a long way, but not enough to make it to Heaven. KIA stands for **K**now **I**t **A**ll. If it is our knowledge that saves us, then it is once again something we possess that saves us. I have a deep desire for people to know the Word of God, but knowing the Word alone will not guarantee eternal life. John 5:39-40 says, "You study the scriptures diligently because you think that in them you have eternal life. These are the very scriptures that testify about Me, yet you refuse to come to Me to have life." They knew it all, but it didn't gain them access into Heaven. Paul also warned Timothy about people who were "always learning but never able to come to a knowledge of the truth" (2 Tim. 3:7). It's a matter of the heart; knowledge of the mind will not save you. There's only one way.

BGTF

I had the opportunity to go to Finland to share this message. When they saw the title—BGTF—they thought it meant "**B**ob **G**oes **T**o **F**inland." But it really stands for **B**y **G**race **T**hrough **F**aith, based on Ephesians 2:8-9: "For it is by grace you have been saved, through faith—and this is not from yourselves, it is the gift of God—not by works, so that no one can boast."

The story goes that God created humankind for relationship with Himself. But our selfishness and our sin has caused a separation between God and people. And nothing we could do can fix that problem or bridge that chasm. The Good News has always been and will always be that God sent His only son, Jesus, who lived and loved perfectly. He then laid down His life on the cross, and three days later rose from the dead. And to anyone who believes in Him is granted the gift of BGTF. My biggest prayer for anyone reading this is that if you have never come to that point, that you would receive His gift by grace through faith.

People were receiving His gift in biblical times too and coming to Christ. The question back then was, "What do we do with these Gentiles who are coming to faith in Christ apart from the law?"

Some of the Pharisees were saying in Acts 15:5, "The Gentiles must be circumcised and required to keep the law of Moses." But Peter said in verse 9, "He [God] did not discriminate between us and them, for He purified their hearts by faith." God purified their hearts by grace through faith (BGTF). He continues in verse 10: "Now then, why do you try to test God by putting on the necks of the Gentiles a yoke that neither we nor our ancestors have been able to bear? *NO!* We believe it is through the grace [BGTF] of our Lord Jesus that we are saved, just as they are." At hearing this, the apostles and the elders met to consider what to do. This historic event has come to be called the Council at Jerusalem. After convening, they said, "It seemed good to the Holy Spirit and to us not to burden you…" (Acts 15:28).

Believers were encouraged in Colossians 2:6: "Just as you received Christ Jesus as Lord, continue to live your lives in Him." It was clear that they had come to salvation by grace, say if you will, saved by grace, but something was happening; something so serious that Paul referred to the Galatians as fools. "I would like to learn just one thing from you," he said. "Did you receive the Spirit [become a Christian] by the works of the law, or by believing what you heard?" (Galatians 3:2). In my Bible I wrote the word "Duh" in the margin next to this passage because it seems so clear. They all knew that they had come to Christ BGTF—by grace through faith.

> For it is by grace you have been saved, through faith—and this is not from yourselves, it is the gift of God—not by works, so that no one can boast (Ephesians 2:8-9).

Paul continued in verse 3, "After starting your new

lives in the Spirit, are you now trying to become perfect by your own human effort?"(NLT). In other words, he was saying, "Hey, what are you doing? You're going backward! You're slipping back. You're backsliding! You started by grace; are you now going back to works?" Paul tells us that the Law was merely given as our tutor, as our guide to lead us to Christ. (See Galatians 3:24.) Later in Galatians 4:9 he says, "But now that you know God—or rather, are known by God—how is it that you are **turning back** to those weak and miserable forces? Do you wish to be **enslaved** by them all over again?" In other words, "Don't put the chains back on!"

Don't look to the Law as a means to earn God's love. It's impossible! That's not why the Law was given. Paul was yelling at them for not believing the promise, but trying to fulfill the Law on their own power, to somehow appease God's wrath and gain His love. He was saying, "Hey, look at the cross! You are loved! You are free! Why are you putting those chains back on?" Galatians 5:1 says that "It is for freedom that Christ has set us free. Stand firm, then [in grace], and do not let yourselves be burdened again by a yoke of slavery." Paul says that if you backslide into trusting in good works, Christ will be of no value to you at all. Then you have to be perfect, obligated to obey the whole Law.

What's the consequence? Paul shows how terrible it is to go back in Galatians 5:4: "You who are trying to be justified by the law have been alienated from Christ; you have fallen away from grace." Backsliding to good works after coming to faith in Jesus is like a dog returning to its own vomit.

IT'S ALL ABOUT GRACE

Thinking about grace and the Christian life brings random but important thoughts to my mind.

Before you were a Christian...

> *Did you live a good enough life to earn Heaven on your own?*
>
> *Yes or no?*
>
> *No.*
>
> *Therefore, your only hope is for a...*
>
> *Gift.*
>
> *Which is called...*
>
> *Grace.*
>
> *What is grace?*
>
> *Unmerited, undeserved favor.*

Since you've been a Christian...

Have you lived a good enough life to earn Heaven on your own?

Yes or no?

No.

Therefore, your only hope is for a...

Gift.

Which is called...

Grace.

What is grace?

Unmerited, undeserved favor.

By the time Jesus comes back (or you die to go be with Him)...

Will you have finally lived a life good enough to earn Heaven on your own?

Yes or no?

No.

Therefore, your only hope is for a...Gift.

Which is called...

Grace.

What is grace?

Unmerited, undeserved favor.

So, it is...

Grace. Grace. Grace.

It's all grace.

It always was.

It always will be.

Old Testament.

New Testament.

Forever.

It's all grace. It's all God.

Do you see it? You start with, continue in, and finish by GRACE.

The truth that proclaims it's only and always by grace is needed today. No matter how long we have walked with Jesus or been in ministry; no matter what we've done for the Kingdom or accomplished in His name, it will still not instill righteousness (right standing with God) on our own. It's like the old saying, "The only righteousness I'll ever have is Christ's; the only sin He'll ever have is mine."

IMPUTED RIGHTEOUSNESS

I'm not big on terminology, and I'm not good at big words, but there's one term I wish every Christian knew: imputed righteousness. Imputed righteousness is a concept in Christian theology which proposes that the righteousness of Jesus Christ satisfies all criteria necessary to share in God's grace. Does our standing with God come from within us, some innate goodness or quality, or does it come from what we do or from our actions? I would yell at the top of my voice, "No!" to both.

The only way we can be in right standing or righteousness is by Christ's merit; not our own. God did for us in Christ what we could not do for ourselves. We can understand the theology of grace in our heads, but not believe it in our hearts, or live it in the day to day, or extend it to ourselves or others. Jesus said that He came to seek and to save sinners. Paul, the lover of the Torah (God's Law) called himself the chief of sinners, because he knew the Law so well, as we all should. Paul saw his need for Jesus.

Only the sick know they need a doctor, and only Dr. Jesus can fix us. We all need more grace, yet I know that some of my own personal drive has kept me so busy that I've looked to my own effort as a measurement for God's approval and others' approval. This shows that I'm still in need of a savior—every day.

Still, when I realize my sin, I think to myself, *I'm the one who blew it. I'm the one who screwed up. I sinned. I should be the one to have to make it right.* I insist that I should have to do penance, and that simple repentance and that turning from my sin is too easy. I think I should have to make up for it and make amends, that if I do enough it will help the feelings of guilt subside. It's as if I'm trying to work out a deal with God. Am I alone here? Have you ever thought this way?

Perhaps you've thought, *God, if You forgive me this sin and don't let it go public, I'll do anything for You; I'll go anywhere; give up whatever; sell and give away anything.* It's almost like saying, "God, I'll pay the fine for breaking Your law. You know, God, like paying for a ticket when I get caught speeding." As if God gives out community service hours as a way to make amends to society! Some of us say no to His grace by insisting, "God, I'll do my own time. Let me spend years in the prison of self-hatred first."

But none of these attempts take care of the problem. Any effort to appease the sentence of God's wrath without receiving what He did for us in His love through Jesus amounts to nothing more than what the Bible calls dead works. (See Hebrews 9:14 KJV.) Admitting that I don't measure up to God's standard is hard enough, but to say I can't and never will be able to, brings me to a whole new level of humility.

So, where is our hope? Our hope is in grace. It's out of my control and I have to depend on Him. All I can do is trust. That is faith. That is true Christianity. If God loves you because of anything you have done or will do, it depends on you, not Him. If this were true, then His love would not be constant—it would fluctuate. If this were true, then Christianity is like all the other religions and we would be required to travel the same broad road as everyone else who thinks their redemption somehow depends on them. No—grace alone sets us apart.

> *Where sin abounded, grace did much more abound* (Romans 5:20 KJV).

Many have said to me, "Bob, it's as if you don't want people to fight against sin, just so they can experience God's grace." That is not what I am saying at all. As a friend of mine, Michael Bridges, said, "I believe in being good. I just wish I could on my own. I can't. It's as if I'm bound in my will to do what's wrong, and the good I want to do, I don't do."

I'm not condoning wrong-doing; I'm just saying I'm not strong enough on my own to conquer sin. My hatred of sin can't conquer it; my hatred of self or the world can't eliminate it. All the books I've read and conferences I've attended didn't achieve it. Every time I've tried on my own, I failed. If it owns me, I just don't have enough to buy sin out. I'm not saying that you should sin more to get more grace. God forbid; may it never be. I'm saying—admit what is still there so you can continue to grow in grace.

ADMIT AND COMMIT

I went to a Bible school through Teen Challenge—a ministry to help addicts break the bondage of drugs and alcohol through Jesus Christ. As part of my training, I had a case load of 10 guys going through the program. Talk about feeling inadequate. I was a college student, just out of high school myself. I was put in charge of helping men who had life-controlling and life-destroying problems. Although young, I knew that to be free these men had to admit that they were in bondage.

> My hatred of sin didn't conquer it; my hatred of self or the world didn't accomplish it. All the books and conferences didn't eliminate it. Every time I've tried on my own, I failed. I'm not saying that you should sin more to get more grace. God forbid; may it never be. I'm saying—admit what is still there so you can continue to grow in grace.

Denial for some is so strong that I'm not sure they even knew they were lying anymore. Facing and dealing with the denial is one of the first steps in anyone's recovery and freedom. These guys were on a work project and were painting some rooms in the facility. Working together was building work habits so they could make it in the real world. Some of the young men in the program told me that one of the guys I had been working with, Todd (not his real name), had been sniffing paint. Addicts will do anything to get another fix. It was my job as his case worker to confront him. If he admitted his wrongdoing, he would face consequences; but if he lied, he would not only face consequences, but would be set back in rank in the program. There was more emphasis placed on being honest and real, than how you messed up.

So I gave Todd a chance to come clean and asked, "Todd, have you been struggling with using any kind of substance at all?"

"No sir, Bob. Nothing," he replied.

"Todd, be honest with me." I wanted to give him every opportunity to confess.

"Honest to God, Bob," he replied earnestly.

"Todd," I continued, "some of the guys saw you sniffing paint. Just own up to it, Todd, and it will go a lot easier for you. It's for your own good. I care, bro, just tell the truth."

He replied with even more conviction and assurance, "Bob, I promise. Maybe those guys are just jealous of me because I'm doing so well. Maybe they're just trying to bring me down. I swear to you; I've not been sniffing paint. I'm doing good with the program and great with God."

What was I, the counselor, supposed to do then? Part of me was so sad, yet part of me wanted to laugh. Why? I gently held Todd's elbow as I escorted him in front of a mirror. He peered into the mirror and saw a ring of paint encircling his entire face where he had put his head into the opening of the can to sniff. His confident posture slowly sunk as he realized his shame. He stared at the reflection that exposed his sin. At first, he chuckled nervously and we shared a short moment of laughter over the absurdity of the moment. But our laughter quickly turned to tears as we realized what it meant.

Until Todd, you, and I are honest with ourselves, we will not experience God's grace. Grace doesn't free us to sin more; it frees us from sin. This is why the church isn't making a bigger difference with the non-churched today. For too long we have acted like we're perfect when all along the world sees the ring of paint around our faces. Most non-churched people today think the church is just a bunch of hypocrites. It's time to look at ourselves in the mirror. Let's not pretend. Let's not deny the sin that remains, but in honesty and humility, admit some of the paint in our lives. It would result in our experiencing God's grace, and allow the world to taste grace through us.

"NO" POWER

Many people see grace as just something we need after we mess up. I'll never forget the story I heard from Don Wilkerson, the international director of Teen Challenge. He talked about a graduate of the program who came back a year after leaving Teen Challenge. As the man sat in Don's office, Don was hoping to hear a victory report.

"Brother Don, I've been out of the program for a year now and I have no power. I have no power over drugs. I have no power over alcohol, and I have no power over lust and premarital sex."

Don's heart fell. He really thought this guy was going to make it. What was puzzling to Don was that there was no remorse in the young man's eyes or on his face. He was almost smiling and Don wondered how he had grown so cold and so hard.

"Isn't that great?" the man said to Don.

Perplexed, Don asked, "What do you mean?"

"God's grace has given me the power to say **no** to drugs, alcohol and sex; **no** to my old way of life. I have '**no**' power, the power to say **no** to sin and **yes** to God."

Is that story awesome, or what? He gets it! Grace isn't just for salvation; it's for living. Grace is for living the Christian life. It empowers us to be who God created us to be. Titus 2:11 tells us, "For the grace of God has appeared that offers salvation to all people." Yes, grace is for salvation, but we need to read on, and go on, in grace.

> It [grace] *teaches us to say* **"No"** *to ungodliness and worldly passions, and to live self-controlled, upright and godly lives in this present age* (Titus 2:12).

Grace gives us **"no"** power, which is real power. It's not a facade. Let me stand by that grace and if I fall, God forbid, may I fall upon His grace and get back up. The Bible says in Proverbs 24:16, "For though the righteous fall seven times, they rise again, but the wicked stumble when calamity strikes." Let's get on with the journey that starts with, continues in, and finishes with grace. I beg you; please don't backslide to your own good works. Walk in, and live by, grace.

REDEEMING GRACE

People have so often said to me, "I wish I'd have heard you when I was young. I wish I had the truth about grace before I messed up my life. I know I'm forgiven and because of God I'll go to Heaven when I die, but what about *this* life? I feel like I've ruined it." Their stories are all different, but the theme is similar: "I have damaged this side of Heaven beyond hope." Those who feel this way, then, do all they can to find sufficient grace to simply endure this life—anticipating complete peace, freedom, and happiness only in the next life.

Please, please, hear me. God is so big and so "grace-full." Even when you were yet unaware of God's great mercy, His mercy was there! Despite your own sin and the atrocities of others' sins against you, remember: Suffering and guilt was never part of God's heart toward you. Know that His love and grace are over it all, and mightier than your pain and despair. Sometimes it seems as if we are standing too close to the painting created by God, the Master Artist. All we see are the dark colors. We're too close to God's creation, to our own life, to see the beauty. We're too close to see how the Artist of our lives can use the darkness in our personal portraits to add depth and character.

For by grace, He redeems the darkness and uses it for our good and His glory. Our redeeming God is a brilliant Artist—and you are His masterpiece. Take a step back and see yourself from His perspective, His vantage point, His eyes – the eyes of grace.

May the grace of our God be with you, now and forever.

CHAPTER 8 DISCUSSION QUESTIONS

1. Why did the Israelites want to go back to slavery in Egypt instead of having freedom in the wilderness?

   • Read Galatians 3:11. How many people will be justified by the law? Why?

2. List the 3 ways you can't get to heaven.

   • GE _____

   • RR _____

   • KIA _____

3. What does BGTF mean? What makes it difficult for you to accept? What makes it easy?

4. What does the chapter title "Backsliding to Good Works" mean?

   • What is your image or definition of a "backslider?"

5. Explain 'dead works' and 'imputed righteousness.'

6. What can you do to get God to love you? Can you do anything that will cause God to love you or cause Him to leave you?

LEADER'S GUIDE

This resource is designed to help leaders delve deeper into the subject of grace. It contains additional questions, topics, and tips to help engage students more fully in discussion. It will allow teachers to explore the importance of grace in their own lives, and to recall stories and illustrations to help students apply what they've learned in the book.

Chapter 1

- Give one or two examples of how you were defiant when you were your students' age. Describe what you were thinking before, during, and after your actions. This transparency and exposure will help develop trust and create an opportunity for them to confide in you. If you weren't rebellious, share why you chose not to be defiant. Walk them through your thought process.

- Discuss how your students feel about church. Carefully listen to them as they voice their concerns. Do you feel that they truly believe they are saved by grace alone?

Remind your students that if we could earn our own salvation, then Jesus' death was in vain, and He died for nothing; we must only accept that He paid the price for our sins.

- Have you ever thought about what the world would be like without you?

    ○ NOTE: If you hear any responses like "Nobody would care if I was gone" or "I wouldn't be missed," these are red flags for you to get help for your student. Negative responses are signs that they feel they aren't fully loved by parents, friends, mentors, and ultimately God. Take your time on this question and help everyone to understand that there would be a massive hole in the world if they were gone, because if that weren't true, God wouldn't have created them. Yet He did, so they are meant to be here.

- In what ways would it change how you judge or treat others if you saw them through eyes of Jesus?

- What does Christ's willingness to offer you the free gift of grace say about your value in His eyes?

- Is it easier for you to see the value of some people more than others? What can you do to help the "Pauls" in your life see their value?

Chapter 2

- Mother Teresa said, "If our poor die of hunger it's not because God does not care for them. Rather, it is because neither you nor I are generous enough. It's because we are not instruments of love in the hands of God."

  ○ How does God want us to treat one another?

  ○ How does this quote blend or conflict with the prior chapter about not having to earn heaven?

    ◊ NOTE: This question can be tricky. The answer is that we need only Jesus, but as Christians we are called to do great things. (See John 14:12, Luke 9:23-24 and Philippians 2:3-4.) When we realize that Jesus says we will do greater things than Him… that should really hit us. It should give us a sense of unwavering strength to tackle any task, any situation, any foe or even the devil himself. But we must first recognize that it isn't by our power at all, but the power of God's Spirit dwelling in us.

Chapter 3

- How do you feel about receiving gifts, getting help from others, or relying on someone else in a desperate time? Which of the following statements more accurately reflects your feelings? (1) "I don't need anyone's help" or (2) "There are many people who have sacrificed to get me to the place I am today."

  - If your answer is number 1, you prefer to be self-reliant and in control. This may reflect a desire to be the god of your own life instead of allowing God to be your God. If you feel like you've done everything in your life on your own, then chances are you don't truly acknowledge that God has provided everything for you. Take some time to decide if you believe this to be true.

  - If your answer is number 2, then you have great wisdom and understanding of who you are, what you've accomplished, what you have, and *whose* you are. But, let's not stop there, let's continue to dig deeper. When was the last time you gave God credit for all the good things happening in your life?

- Think about Callie's story for a moment. Are your students fully aware of the fact that God is watching over them? Are you? Can you think of times when you forgot to thank God for his help?

- This chapter contains the quote, "The proudest people I know are also the most insecure." Here is an opportunity to set aside pride and insecurity and engage in complete candor. Open up to your students about the ways you feel inadequate. Share about times when you questioned whether God could ever use you, and what happened.

Chapter 4

- This chapter mentions modern-day Pharisees. Ask your students whether they feel that Christians tend to behave more like Pharisees or Jesus. Are they known more for what they stand against, or for how loving they are?

- Can you define the focus, the intent, purpose, and drive of your heart?

- Is Christ at the center of your world? When has God been "number one" in your life, and when have you pushed him aside?

- Has your passion and personal relationship with Jesus been replaced with a focus on morality?

- Share with your students some ways they can refresh and strengthen their relationship with Jesus.

Chapter 5

- What were some of your thoughts after reading this chapter?

  ○ Note: This chapter is written like a poetic collage of thoughts and feelings about the life-long process of experiencing and understanding God's unconditional love. Most of the chapter reads like many of the Psalms, expressing sin's accusations and consequences, human questions, apathy, judgement, and finally the Gospel's healing and life-giving power to forgive, restore, and transform. Highlight some of the statements that reflect your own feelings. Share honestly about your own "collage." Tell your students about moments you felt far from God or very close to Him and why.

- How often does self-doubt arise when you reflect on the intensity of your relationship with God?

- How does our Savior's description of love contrast with what we see in our world? (See John 15:13)

Chapter 6

- What do you think about the conversation with the camp counselor who said, "You're not a Christian yet. You're not a saint; you're still a sinner?" Discuss what it feels like to receive this kind of harsh judgment, and explore how people experience salvation.

- Being a Christian is a life-long journey of repenting and responding to Jesus' love. Experiencing God's grace and forgiveness is not a one-time occurrence because a Christian can never fully stop sinning. We often find ourselves wanting to stop, yet still indulging in the same familiar sin. What sins are holding you captive? Do you need to remember that 1 John 1:9 says that He **will** forgive you (not **might** forgive you)?

  ○ Martin Luther said we need to "daily drown our old Adam." In other words, we need to kill off our old sinful self each day. Remind your students that who we were yesterday is not who we are today in Christ Jesus. We are made new (2 Corinthians 5:17); we are alive in him today because of what He did for us.

- Has your relationship with God become simply a weekly routine... a tradition of going to church? Do you feel forced to attend? If not, what motivates you to go?

Chapter 7

- C.S. Lewis asked, "Why must holy places be dark places?" Share how some of the hardest times you have gone through in your personal life have brought glory to God or have drawn you closer to Him or others.

- Share with your students some of the "dark places" in your heart. The Bible tells us that if we claim we have no sin, we deceive ourselves and the truth is not in us; but if we confess our sins, God, who is faithful and just, will forgive our sins (1 John 1:9). Acknowledge some of your struggles and explain what you have done about them.

- How many times have you tried to gain grace on your own power, yet failed? Can you think of examples?

- Challenge yourself and your students with this question: Are you ready to admit where and who you really are, even if you're not where you wish you were, or where others think you are?

Chapter 8

- GE: Can you ever be "good enough" to inherit the kingdom of God?

- RR: Will traveling the "religious road" take you to heaven? Will going to church, saying your prayers, and performing religious rituals guarantee you a spot?

- KIA: Does it gain you points with God if you "know it all?" Will knowing scripture backwards and forwards earn you a ticket into the heavenly gates? Or do you want to know God's Word to get to know Him better?

- Do you feel like you have no power? Or do you have **'No'** power? Share a story of victory over temptation (whether big or small... your story or someone else's), and help your students understand that when they are faced with a choice between doing the right thing or the wrong thing, they can pray and ask God to give them the power to say 'No'.

ENDORSEMENTS

Bob Lenz' moving work called "Grace: For those who think they don't measure up" is not only a well-crafted book of Biblical insight for the hearts and minds of young people today, it is an important and compelling offering of encouragement to untold numbers of people who are bewildered with life, bereft of encouragement and bankrupt of hope.

Bob's focus on Jesus' passion to save us and give us life through His merits and sacrifice alone are indeed the sum and substance of Bob's true expression of Grace. This book is suitable for quiet nights of private contemplation as well as a text for a confirmation classroom. It breathes fresh air into the deep places of people's lives where they work, play, live, love, think and feel.

Knowing Bob's zest to bring the Good News of Jesus into young people's hearts through his passionate messages and memorable storytelling as a headline speaker, this book allows the eye to take in what many ears and hearts have already received. Ferociously committed to God's Word, Bob's thoughts, insights and teachings offer sound, orthodox theology as well as contemporary illustrations that many will find applicable to their lives and situations.

Not only is this book a must-read for pastors, teachers and Christian leaders, it should have a place on every library shelf for reference and continued encouragement. For me, it remains a resource for teaching, an encouragement in contemplation and a beacon light of hope amid the dark tomes of new-age philosophies and non-Biblical theologies.

Pastor Bill Yonker
Senior Pastor, Immanuel Lutheran Church

Take a deep breath of hope, and prepare to set sail for deeper waters in this remarkable exploration of God's truly amazing gift of grace! This book will both challenge and encourage you in your spiritual journey.

Rebecca St. James
Grammy-winning Christian singer
and best-selling author

With humor, insight, grit, and power, Bob Lenz has done it again! This is a take-no-prisoners-make-no-excuses-drag'em-laughing-and-kicking-to-Jesus book that's worth your time investment on every page.

Rev. Rich Melheim
Founder and Chief Creative Officer
Faith Inkubators, www.faithink.com

Bob Lenz is a passionate man, a brilliant communicator, and a troubled man—troubled enough to know that he needs grace more than he needs air, water, or food. We desperately need grace—we can never know the fullness of what God's delight means for us. We desperately need to be invited to the wildness of God's love by an equally wild person. Bob disturbs the self-righteous and simultaneously comforts the heavy-ladened—and we are all both to some degree. May this glorious book take you in its arms so you can hear the song sung to you by our passionate God.

Dan B. Allender, PhD
President, Mars Hill Graduate School
Author, *To Be Told, The Wounded Heart*

Bob Lenz really nails it in this great little book. Grace is a gift, pure and simple. He eloquently "makes his case" with beautiful examples and clear logic, based upon and backed up by Scripture. It is a liberating experience to read these pages. Salvation is not complicated. It cannot be earned by good works or anything else. It is God's free gift, through Christ. Grab hold and give thanks, both for this book and for God's grace.

Millard Fuller
Founder, Habitat for Humanity
Founder and President, The Fuller Center
for Housing

Like a prism shining in the sunlight, Bob Lenz has creatively and effectively shown us the many facets of God's amazing grace. With integrity and respect, he has peeled back the layers of misconceptions that exist in the church today to proclaim the life-giving truth of Christ's death and resurrection. *Grace* is a compelling wake-up call for the church as it embarks on the 21st century. It is genuine, entertaining…truly written from the heart!

Patra S. Mueller
Family Life Minister, Hope Lutheran Church, Seattle, WA
Former Assistant Professor of Christian Education
Concordia University, Irvine, California

If you have ever heard Bob Lenz address a crowd, he always holds them spellbound. I have seen our festival crowd hang on every word. Grace brings excitement and inspired truth to the reader. If you want an unpredictable wild ride of grace with God, this book is for you.

Rev. Dr. Harry L. Thomas
Director and Cofounder
Creation Festivals East/West and Friendship Fest, Morocco

I work in a faith-based, grace-based ministry. I thought I'd learned much about the grace of God and its application to the lost and hurting. However, Bob's book has opened the eyes of my understanding even deeper and wider to what amazing grace is all about. This is a book I wish I'd written. The reader will be glad Bob has given the Body of Christ another look at this inexhaustible subject. It's written in a contemporary style with absolutely no compromise of the Gospel of Jesus Christ. Read it, apply it, and pass it along to others. I highly recommend *Grace*.

Don Wilkerson
Executive Director/Founder
Global Teen Challenge

In this book, Bob Lenz offers us a challenge to get over ourselves and get into a place where we recognize that God's love for us is deeper than anything we can comprehend. Building on over 20 years of helping youth and adults come to know about this love, Bob gets right to the point: God's grace is enough! God's grace is the reason for our existence; God's grace is what sets us free; God's grace is what compels us to love and serve our brothers and sisters. It is God's grace that makes us measure up.

Rich Curran
Founder and Executive Director of Parish Success Group
Former Director of Youth and Young Adult Ministry
Diocese of Green Bay

In a world that is increasingly confused about spiritual truth, my friend, Bob Lenz, cuts to the heart of the matter with a crystal clear focus on "grace." He has poured his heart, his mind, and his experience as an evangelist into a thorough and highly practical look at how grace changes lives. Bob takes you from your experience of law and grace and delivers you into a deeper understanding that touches the mind and the heart. It's great news for the weary—and a wake-up call for the legalist.

Dr. Wess Stafford
President Emeritus
Compassion International

RECOMMENDED RESOURCES

Books on Grace that have impacted Bob Lenz

The Bible

Grace Awakening
by Chuck Swindoll

What's So Amazing About Grace
by Phillip Yancey

Abba's Child
by Brennan Manning

In the Grip of Grace
by Max Lucado

Commentary on Galatians
by Martin Luther

The Proper Distinction Between Law and Gospel
by Dr. C.F. Walther

ABOUT THE AUTHOR

Bob Lenz connects with more than 500,000 people each year through various speaking events, and each year thousands respond to the gospel message of hope and grace. Bob explores sober real-life issues while using his unique gift of humor. Somewhere between the uproarious laughter over an embarrassing moment or the hushed silence of a touching story, young people realize their lives have been changed.

Bob works closely with public and private school districts providing effective assembly programs, speaking clearly on values, courage, respect, and the importance of making good choices. Often, students have an opportunity to attend an evening community outreach after Bob speaks in their school. Bob shares his faith and the message of God's grace and unconditional love. More than five million people have heard Bob speak at events such as evangelistic rallies, professional conferences, festivals, schools, youth leader training, and state and national church events.

Bob is president and founder of Life Promotions; a nonprofit ministry whose mission is to reach young people with the gospel before they turn 18 years of age. In addition to speaking professionally, Bob served as a youth pastor, director of a counseling center, and hosted a Christian radio program. Bob's formal education was through Teen Challenge Ministry Institute.

Bob also founded Lifest, one of the nation's largest Christian music festivals held each summer in Oshkosh, Wisconsin. The event includes more than 100 acts on six stages along with family activities, seminars and camping. Visit lifest.com for more details.

Although speaking is a great privilege for Bob, his first commitment is to his family. His wife Carol, five children and several grandchildren are sources of great joy and unending examples of committed love.

More information on Bob Lenz, including upcoming speaking engagements, booking information and resources, can be found at LifePromotions.com or by calling 800-955-5433.

OTHER BOOKS BY BOB LENZ

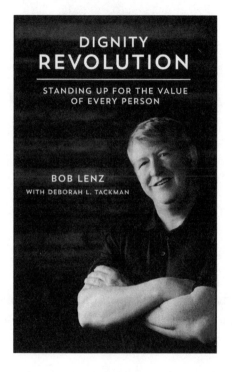

Dignity Revolution: Standing Up for the Value of Every Person

A comprehensive book on bullying. Bob Lenz teamed up with Deborah Tackmann, B.S., M.E.P.D, to tackle one of the most important issues of our day. *Dignity Revolution* brings to the forefront what life could be for all of us when every person is valued and offered dignity.

This is Life: Real Stories from the Road

Twenty-five true short stories from the travels of Bob Lenz, sharing joy and triumph, hurt and heartache, and most of all…hope.

Books available at *LifePromotions.com*

Book Bob Lenz to speak at your next school assembly program or youth event!

Visit www.lifepromotions.com
Phone: 800-955-5433

Follow Bob on Social Media

facebook.com/boblenz.lifepromotions/

twitter.com/boblenzLIFE
@boblenzlife

instagram.com/boblenzlife/
boblenzlife

"My relationship with Maykin, the boy I sponsor in Haiti, is releasing him from poverty in Jesus' name."
– Bob Lenz

COMPASSION
INTERNATIONAL

To sponsor a child through Compassion, go to:
www.compassion.com/bob-lenz

DIGNITY REVOLUTION

Educating and Empowering Youth to Stand up for the Value of Every Person

The Dignity Revolution Challenge, a customizable bullying prevention program, was created by Deborah L. Tackmann (2012 National Health Teacher of the Year), Bob Lenz, and a team of experienced teachers.

It was created based on the belief that students can change the world and that a simple encounter with love can motivate students to treat others with dignity and respect.

Start a Dignity Revolution in your community.

DignityPledge.com

QUAKE

YOUTH ENCOUNTERING THE **GOSPEL**

Life Promotions hosts Quake events, weekend conferences across the U.S. for Christian youth groups, grades 6-12. Quake helps youth become established in their Christian faith, empowered for Christian living, and encouraged to live a life of ministry and Christian leadership. This is accomplished through interactive worship, large and small group activities, and relational ministry.

Relational ministry at Quake begins as informal conversations that grow authentic relationships between youth, adult leaders, and staff. As relationships deepen, trust and care is established, faith is shared, and faith formation flourishes through the work of the Holy Spirit.

Visit LifePromotions.com/Quake for information on upcoming Quake events in your area.

A PARTY WITH A **PURPOSE**

JULY • OSHKOSH WI • LIFEST.COM

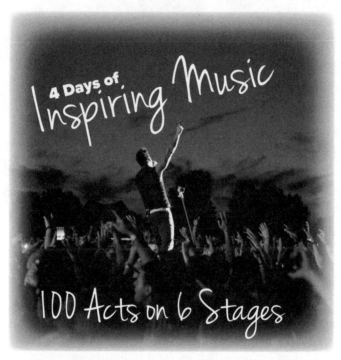

4 Days of Inspiring Music

100 Acts on 6 Stages

One of the Nation's Largest Christian Music Festivals

Comedians • Seminars • Camping
Art Space • 5K Run • KidZone
And so much more!

<18>

FAITH FOR THE
NEXT GENERATION

Join Bob Lenz to Bring Hope to America's Youth
Become a monthly <18> supporter today.
LifePromotions.com/Donate

NOTES

NOTES

NOTES